ECX AND THE WINDS OF CHANGE

A MEMOIR FROM ETHIOPIA

DR. BHARAT KULKARNI

Made with ♥ on the Notion Press Platform
www.notionpress.com

Contents

Disclaimer

The following memoir, "ECX and the Winds of Change: A memoir from Ethiopia," is a deeply personal and introspective account of the experiences, thoughts, and emotions of the author. The content presented within these pages is based on the author's recollections and reflections up to the time of writing.

It is important to note that memory can be subjective and may evolve over time. Events, conversations, and details recounted in this memoir are based on the author's perspective and understanding, which may differ from the perspectives of others who were present during the same situations. While the author has made every effort to present an accurate and honest portrayal of their life, some names, locations, and identifying characteristics may have been altered or omitted to protect the privacy and anonymity of individuals.

This memoir is not intended to provide professional advice, therapeutic guidance, or factual documentation of historical events. It is a narrative work of art that captures the essence of the author's experiences and should be interpreted as such.

Readers are encouraged to approach this memoir with an open heart and mind, understanding that the emotions and insights shared are a part of the author's personal journey. The author and publisher disclaim any liability for interpretations, actions, or consequences that readers may derive from the content of this memoir.

DISCLAIMER

By engaging with "ECX and the Winds of Change: A memoir from Ethiopia," readers acknowledge and accept the subjective nature of personal recollection and the artistic intent of the author. Your understanding and respect for the author's narrative perspective are greatly appreciated.

Foreword

Africa normally gives an impression of a poor ,war ridden , desert dominated continent with low level of education and technology. This is so wrong. I had similar opinion of Africa when posted to Ethiopia as the country head of Tata International. Every country has her challenges and Ethiopia is no different, but these can be handled and solved like in any other developing economy. Meeting new people and knowing their heritage and culture is so enriching. This is in addition to huge business opportunities in the region .

I met Bharat in the Indian Embassy in 2009 at the Republic Day function. A pleasant surprise to meet some from my hometown Indore in Madhya Pradesh. Soon we were very close and started sharing professional and personal challenges and accomplishments. Our PP partnership that he talks about was something we really enjoyed.

This is so good to see that Bharat has decided to share his experience of setting up the first agricultural commodity exchange in the African region.

Structural trading platform for a large agricultural economy is so important for the farmers and the economy of the country. This provides transparency and ease in trade and creates wealth for the farmers and the country. There could not been have a better time to build ECX in Ethiopia. Bharat with his hands on experience at MCX India had the right knowledge to take on this task.

His youthfulness , drive and strong desire to succeed and his hardworking enthusiastic team made ECX a great success . ECX now stands as an example and benchmark for the rest of Africa and the developing world.

I am certain that this compilation in the form of a book will provide great insights for the professionals , bureaucrats and development agencies to take on such projects around the world.

By

Sushil Dubey

Acknowledgements

Writing a memoir is a deeply personal and reflective journey, and I am grateful to have completed this book with the support, love, and encouragement of so many incredible individuals. It is with immense joy and humility that I extend my heartfelt acknowledgments to the following people:

To my mother, Mrs. Hemangini Kulkarni, and my father, S.K.B. Kulkarni, who provided unwavering support throughout my life, I am forever grateful. Your love and understanding have been a beacon of strength in my life. My mother, for traveling all the way to Addis Ababa from India, her first international travel at the age of 63, for learning to use emails to remain in touch with me, and for many more

To my dear Wife, Runa Kulkarni, your unwavering belief in me and your patience during our initial days in Addis Ababa have been invaluable. I know how difficult it was for you to move to Addis and navigate through those initial days! Your love and encouragement have sustained me through the ups and downs of our days in Addis Ababa and throughout my life. You are my rock, and I am deeply blessed to have you by my side.

To my dear daughter, whose love for writing at such a young age has encouraged me to write this memoir. I wanted to do it for the past ten years, but I was lazy, I guess. Your motivation made it possible for me.

To my circle of friends who have listened to me, offered feedback, and cheered me on, I am deeply thankful. Your friendship and camaraderie have enriched my life in countless ways, and I am fortunate to have you all as a constant source of inspiration. Especially those from Addis Ababa, including my colleagues of that time, you gave me those memories that made it worth writing.

To the publishing team of Notion Press that worked tirelessly behind the scenes to bring this book to life, I am grateful for your passion and commitment to the written word.

Finally, I acknowledge the very process of writing this memoir. It has been a transformative experience, filled with moments of reflection, growth, and self-discovery. I am grateful for every challenge and triumph, as they have shaped me into the person I am today.

Writing a memoir is a labour of love that would not have been possible without the support and love of so many remarkable individuals. Your belief in me and my story have carried me through this journey, and for that, I am forever thankful.

CHAPTER ONE

The Beginning

Trin-Trin, my phone started to ring as my bus was getting close to my office. I was working for Multi Commodity Exchange (MCX) by then and used to take a bus daily from Thane, where I had shifted few months back, to my office at Andheri east. I picked up the phone and it was my old friend and current colleague Nitin Joshi (Now Dr Nitin Joshi) on the other side. Dr Nitin was working with me in the training department, and was in charge of working with the academic institutes. Currently he was out in Indore for a meeting with the IIM-Indore. He was accompanied by our boss – Dr Chiragra Chakrabary, vice president for training. “Hi Joshi ji!” I said as I picked up the call. I was surprised as Dr Nitin had just gone to Indore day before yesterday, and was calling me much before the office hours. I was sure it was definitely nothing related to office work. Dr Nitin and me knew each other since 2002. I had recommended him to join MCX in 2006. He suddenly asked me what is the status of your passport ? Is your passport there with you? I was perplexed with the question as this was very much out of context. I had no idea what Dr Nitin was talking about and more importantly why he was asking me about my passport?

I told him “well, my passport has some issues and there is a query which I need to resolve before getting the passport”. I had applied for my passport earlier but the passport was not delivered to me. Now I had to go to the Passport Office, and collect the passport. Dr Nitin’s question was a total surprise to me. I asked him what had happened, and why was he asking me about my passport? He told me that today sometime morning Dr Chiragra is going to call me and ask me about my passport. So, before I get surprised by his question, he thought he’ll just let me know that such a question is coming. I asked him about the context in which Dr Chiragra was going to ask me. He shared with me that yesterday when both of them were together, Dr Chiragra had received a call from Ethiopia and there is a training program to be conducted in Ethiopia where my name has been suggested by the Ethiopians. However, Dr Chiragra seems to be more inclined towards sending someone else from the team. So, if I tell him that I don’t have the passport, he might use that to convey the Ethiopians that I do not have passport and as a result cannot travel. I was not surprised.

I thanked Nitin bhai and started thinking about my passport and the way I will get it issued from Bhopal. As expected, within few hours Dr Chiragra called and asked me the same question "Do you have a passport "very casually and without context. I was as prepared for it as Tendulkar used to be for the pitched-up deliveries! I immediately told him that my passport is issued but have to collect it from the Bhopal passport office. It was the safest answer I could give Chiragra. He told me to go to Bhopal and get the passport issued before the end of this week, as I might have to go to Ethiopia in next week.

As Dr Chiragra went offline, memories started to flashback for February that year, when a delegation from Ethiopia had come to India for a one month-long training program. After a lot of back and forth, a bunch of Ethiopians, approximately thirty in number, came to India to understand and get trained on the commodity exchange concepts. The delegation was led by a charismatic lady, Dr Eleni Gabre-madhin, a senior economist from Ethiopia. With her, a person called Bemnet Aschenaki aka Ben was also there. For few days a third person, Messseret Nega also joined. Little did I knew that they would be my colleagues in less than a year's time. The training of Ethiopians in India was an experience in itself.

The call from Dr Nitin was important for me as it had alerted me about the opportunity coming and I had to ensure I do not miss it. I was working for MCX by the, in the training department, and was in charge of conducting training programs, specifically for the agricultural sector. After the call, the important priority was to get the passport. I travelled to Bhopal and with the help of one of my neighbour Harish Bhaiya, was able to get the passport. Unaware of the process, I was confused and worried. My mother spoke to one of our neighbour, Harish bhaiya, casually about it and he offered help. He knew someone in Bhopal who was well versed with the process and tasked him to help me to smoothly navigate through the process, that too quickly. It was his help that I managed to get my passport issued in time.

With the passport in my hand, I was now ready to travel to Ethiopia. Ethiopia, for that matter was a lesser-known country in those days, at least to me. The travel was approaching and we had to secure our visas and prepare for the travel in less than a week. This was my first international travel and I was pretty excited to get a visa stamped. With the help of our Ethiopian friends, as it was a government of Ethiopia project, managed to get the Ethiopia embassy issue the visa immediately same day. The visa was to be issued from Delhi, as by then the Ethiopian Consulate in Mumbai had not opened. Our travel desk suggested that the easiest and the most convenient way to get the visa in time was to fly into Delhi with passports, get the visa stamped and returned to Mumbai. As our travel was fixed for Saturday, we decided to send someone with the three passports – mine, Shaivalya Thacker's and Ankan Mondal's, the travelling team, to get the visa from Delhi. Youngest of the three, Ankan Mondal volunteered to fly into Delhi with all the necessary documents and get the visa approved. I was waiting anxiously to see how the visa would look. By Wednesday, the visa was in my hand.

Our colleague, Shaivalya's wife is a doctor, and in course of discussion she got to know that there is a yellow fever vaccination mandatory for everyone travelling to Ethiopia. I had never heard Yellow Fever and was a bit worried. As anyways, Africa is always perceived to be land of unknown aliments and mystery around Africa made me more worried. However, it was to be taken and vaccination centres were only either the Ballard Pier in Mumbai or at the Chhatrapati Shivaji Maharaj International Airport health centre. Still the vaccination requirement continues.

However, we reached the International Airport, only to realise that the vaccination is only limited in number per day! And, if you are lucky, then only you get it same day. The health centre, in those days in 2007, was a very basic facility and they would give only sixty shots a day. For this, hundreds of people would line up. One has to register his/her name on a paper, which the clerk from the Health Centre would come up with an hour before 3 p.m. . That used to be the time when they would start giving the shots. Once the sixty shots are over for the day, its done. We were praying that we should get shot as we were also worried knowing that the vaccination could cause dizziness or some kind of fever or nausea. We did not want to get into the travel day with any such issue. Luckily somehow, I, Shaivalya and Ankan, managed to get vaccination in our second attempt on Thursday.

With that out of list, I was ready for my first international travel, knowing little that this is just a beginning. We were booked on Ethiopian Airlines flight, an airline which I never knew existed before I saw the ticket of Ethiopian Airlines. The flight was to take off at 5:40 a.m. on Sunday and reach Addis Ababa the capital city of Ethiopia-our destination at 8 a.m. local time. Since it was an international flight for the first time in my life I was excited and left home at midnight. Never did I knew that these midnight fights would start to be so agonizing and painful in coming years.

Those days, we did not have Ola or Ubers. Only thing you depended upon was the Black-Yellow cab, or the kaali peeli as it is called in Mumbai, to go to the airport those days. My house in thane was, in those days, a bit remote, finding a taxi that two p.m. in the night was absolutely impossible. The best way was to call up the taxi association office at the mulund check naka and ask them to come to pick you up. I called the taxi, and after picking up the package of books to be taken along, reached the International Airport in time.

I was unknown to the concept of extra luggage. I and Shaivalya were carrying a bulky package of the study materiel. Both of us did not know that travellers traveling together can add up their luggage allowance. Both of us had forty kg luggage allowance and we were carrying bags not more than twenty kgs. each. However, we had a big package of books which weighed around thirty to forty kgs. in itself. As we went to the counters separately, for checking in, I was told that total weight I am carrying is in excess of the allowed allowance. I will have to pay for extra luggage. The guy at the counter (who later became a manager) told me that I should give him $100 and he will let go all the weight without measuring it. But in that case, we will not get a receipt. I consulted Shaivalya and we agreed that for us to get reimbursement from the company, it was important to take the receipt. I told him to charge as per the rules and give me the receipt. He charged me for fifteen kg excess baggage, whereas Shaivalya was having twenty kg of ideal allowance! But neither Shaivalya, nor me knew to use that allowance. Well it was the first and the last time that I was schemed for extra luggage at airport.

As per the plan agreed with the Ethiopian clients, I was required to stay for three weeks and Shaivalya would return after ten days. He would be replaced by our third colleague Ankan, who would stay with me for another ten days. I was considering myself lucky that my boss has given me an opportunity to have an extended stay in Ethiopia. It was few years later, that Ben told me that he had put the condition that either me or Shaivalya should stay for three weeks, otherwise this training program is cancelled. Since Shaivalya was adamant not to stay for three weeks the only option left for my boss was to keep me there for three weeks. Though Chiragra kept pushing for Aknan, Ben was adamant for me.

One must be wondering why an Ethiopian would put a condition ? The answer is in the first visit of Ethiopians to India. In February 2007, MCX JMD Lamon Rutten, a global stalwart in the commodity exchange sector and a wonderful human being, was helping Dr Eleni in putting together the **Ethiopia Commodity Exchange (ECX)**. It was his insistence, that the Ethiopians had agreed to come to India for a paid training program. This was to be conducted by MCX. I was in charge of that training program and designed and manage the whole training program. During the training program, I developed a very strong bond with the Ethiopian counterparts.

Having thirty Ethiopian participants in Mumbai for four weeks was an amazing experience for all of us. We had planned an elaborate training program for them where they would understand the basics of the commodity exchange and see how that can be used in Ethiopia. By then Ethiopia had already started to work on establishment of the commodity exchange, led by Dr Eleni gabre-madhin and her two team members, Bemnet (Ben) Aschenaki and Messeret Nega. It was during this period Ben and I developed mutual respect for each other's knowledge and a good friendship, that is still very strong.

Food habits are often derived from culture. In Ethiopia, coffee is not a drink, but a part of culture. First time that I realised this and experienced how much Ethiopian love their coffee was during their stay in India. Till then I was oblivious to the fact that Ethiopia is one of the major producers of coffee and coffee is so integral to the local culture of Ethiopia. The Ethiopian delegation was staying in a MTNL training facility in Powai in Mumbai. The daily breakfast, lunch and dinner was prepared and served by the caterer. The caterer would, in the morning breakfast as well as in the afternoon, offer tea and coffee. In India, unless you are in South India, coffee is instant coffee. However, Ethiopians consider the instant coffee as chemical! Disappointed by the coffee, they would ask the caterer to put high amount of instant coffee powder in the coffee cup.

The caterer reused after a day saying that it was disturbing his cost planning. If you ask any caterer, while costing it is considered s more of tea and some coffee. Not very sure, but something like 3:1 ratio. Since everybody was drinking coffee, that too with coffee powder sufficient for 4-5 cups, put in one cup, his cost of catering is going up and he bc compensated for it. This went on for few days, after which one of the Ethiopian participants travelled from Ethiopia to India, brought coffee from Ethiopia for them to enjoy in India. This made, both caterers and the participants happy.

Foreigners in India have very many types of experiences. Some good, sometime, unfortunately, bad. One such incident, while these Ethiopians were in India, I remember was with one of the participants called Bulbula Tuly. Bulbula was a very reputed businessman, dealing into oilseeds and pulses, and was in India as part of the training team. In the evenings, most of the participants would go to different shopping malls and shopping centres for shopping. On one of such shopping visits, Bulbula forgot his passport and his wallet in a rickshaw. The rickshaw driver was a very honest fellow and wanted to return the documents and the money. But since it was money, he was afraid that he might be accused of stealing some money out of the wallet. Here, at the training centre, Bulbula was very upset as he had lost his passport. As we were trying to figure out a solution, the local police station reached out to us and told us that the rickshaw driver has come to the station with the documents and the wallet. They told us to bring Bulbula to collect it. As the rickshaw driver was afraid, he had reached out to a local politician who took him to the police, assuring him that he would not be in trouble. Bulbula, very happy by now wanted to give some tip to the rickshaw driver. However, he refused saying it was his duty. This image of India Bulbula still carries with him.

Coming back to our flight to Ethiopia, it was comfortable and we landed at 8 a.m., local time. It was my first international travel and I was pretty excited. In that excitement, I did not realise how the five hours of travel time passed. As we landed in Addis Ababa, and came out after our immigration and collecting the baggage, we were greeted by a very pleasant and beautiful weather of Addis Ababa. Till now, my conception about Ethiopia and Africa as a whole, was that Africa was of hot place with the irritating weather. Soon on arrival I realised how wrong I was and the weather in Addis is very pleasant comfortable.

The training arrangements were done by International Food Policy Research Institute (IFPRI), where the project of setting up the ECX was housed. IFPRI driver Solomon, who in coming times would become a good friend, picked us up from the airport and took us to the most iconic Hotel of yester years in Addis Ababa. This was the Ghion hotel. It is an old palatial hotel with nice interiors and a very nostalgic look. Back in the times of Dergu, this was the most iconic hotel in Addis Ababa. I and Shaivalya were assigned our rooms 606 and 607. Both of us, feeling a need to catch up some sleep, went to our rooms quickly. Entering the room, I did not see any fan. I immediately asked the attendant "where's the fan?" He very coolly responded "no fan sir". Confused, I asked again "then there must be an AC", to which he said "no, no AC." Now I was a bit more confused how can I stay in a room with without a fan or an AC. I again asked him "if I feel hot, what do I do?" He very coolly said "open the windows". I was getting a bit irritated, thinking how can opening a window be the solution? He opened the window for me and I said let me see what happens. I was too tired and immediately went to sleep. Within half an hour, I realised what he meant. The room had become freezing cold, as if somebody had switched on the AC. Welcome to Addis

Ababa, a city with wonderful weather where you feel the weather is naturally air-conditioned

I closed the window and went to sleep. I got up at around 2 p.m. in the afternoon, as we were to go for a reception at the ECX office at 3 p.m.. Solomon came to take us to the ECX office. After briefly meeting Eleni in India, this was my first meeting with Dr Eleni in Addis. Also, we were welcomed by few members from the team who had come to India. They had come there and meet us over a drink. As always, I took a coke and was very happy to meet all the old friends. I must say the affection and respect they showed to us was so encouraging.

While returning to the hotel, it was late evening and Addis was getting cold. I spoke to Shaivalya about the weather and he told me that he had taken his shirt out of his bag and hung it on the window so that he can wear it for the evening meeting. However, because the window was open, the shirt became so cold that he could not even wear it. Shaivalya was born and brought up in Mumbai, so cold was so alien to him.

We were in Ethiopia to conduct a three-week workshop on commodity markets as Ethiopia was building its own commodity exchange. This workshop was part of the capacity building program that the United Nations Development Program (UNDP) was financing for the Ethiopian government to develop capacity in the market for commodity exchange. Most of the participants were from the business and academic fraternity. After the conduction of a successful training program in February that year, this was the second in the line and was conducted in Ethiopia for the first time. The program was conducted at the place that the ECX had rented to build its office and trading floor. one of the participants who had attended training program in India was Mulugeta Gabre-Madhin. He was a professor at the Addis Ababa Commercial college and was to be the training head for ECX. He was one of the trainees that we had trained and was to take a few sections in the second round of training as a part of capacity building. He was very diligent in scheduling and would keep sending messages to us about time. He would ensure the participants follow the time so that we start on time and end on time.

When this training program was being designed, the challenge was, that we had to make a two-day training program long enough for three weeks. Though some new sessions were added but the old sessions had to be deliberated in more detail and it was there that my understanding about the agricultural markets and my time spent with friends in the agriculture mandi in India came very handy. Shaivalya was a gold expert and was very good in structured markets for gold, but when it came to agriculture, he had his own limitations. Though I have learnt a lot from him, but in the agriculture sector, he would look up to me. I still remember an incident where I had to speak about delivery concept in maize contract for one and half hour. I was going word by word, line by line explaining each, what it meant and why it was important. I guess, those sessions were more useful for me then the participants. I got more and more convinced in the coming days, months and years.

Another incident I could recollect was at the first day lunch. I and Shaivalya were confused looking at the first dish that was kept immediately after as we picked up the dishes. It a very neatly rolled piece, which looked like a napkin to me. I could not understand, neither could Shaivalya, what this was. Confused, we skipped it to pick the bread and some salad as our lunch. Both of us being vegetarian, we had our own challenges in terms of food. I being an indori and Shaivalya being a gujarati, we missed our food all the more. However, I was keenly looking at what this roll was. I had my belief that this was a napkin kept to clean hands, but then. the colour was very pale brownish, rather than white. I asked to myself why would somebody keep such a dusty coloured napkin? As I was having these questions, to my surprise, I saw people picking it up and putting it in their plates. Everybody was using it as a roti to eat it with the curries. Ethiopian food is very much like Indian food, which has lot of curries and use of spices. This roll was their staple food called Injera. It is very close to the dosa that we make in South India. Only thing is it is made out of teff flour. Teff is a gluten-free grain grown in Ethiopia. It is the staple diet of the country. This was my first experience with injera and Ethiopian food.

I somehow sustain the first day and we returned to our hotel by around 4 in the evening. We needed some rest, as we were feeling too tired. We were wondering why are we feeling tired? Then we realised that the altitude at which Addis Ababa is situated, makes availability of oxygen less and tires you much earlier than you would in Mumbai. So, every day after our return we would go back to the hotel take some rest and then reassemble for our dinner in the restaurant at the Gihon. The restaurant used to serve only Ethiopian traditional food with some choices of spaghetti.

However Ethiopian food is highly dominated by beef, and we both being strict vegetarians, found it very difficult. Finally, we found something that we could eat. We identified white rice and Shiro. Shiro is an Ethiopian traditional dish, very similar to dall. It is made from chickpeas. Also, we could get misser, made from masur or red lentils. Like India, Ethiopian food also has a very high usage of lentils. Shiro is part of their staple diet. Injera Shiro is something that every Ethiopian eats twice a day. I called the waiter and told him to bring rice and shiro. As I told him, he took a deep breath as if he had hiccups. I asked him if he was okay. He said yes and then I told him also bring two coke with it. He again had a hiccup.

I was genuinely worried about him and I told him he should get some water. He looked at me confused and just smiled. After having our dinner, I asked the waiter to bring the bill for us and he again had a hiccup. I didn't understand if he was doing it purposely or was genuinely in trouble. We paid the bill and went back to our rooms. Next day, we had the same experience with another guy. I could not hold back, and asked my friend Ben about these hiccups. He laughed and told me that it is the way of saying yes in Ethiopia! That was my first time that I realised that Ethiopian while speaking if they have a hiccup it indicates that they are saying yes or agreeing or saying they understand. Very interesting

I am Shaivalya used to fight it out every day at the training program as both of us had a competition of giving the best. One thing I appreciated about Shaivalya was he was someone who would always try for excellence and would bring a lot of positive energy and commitment to the work. Those the days with Shaivalya were exciting and very encouraging. As we reached the end of week, we were tired of eating rice shiro and decided to explore Indian restaurant Ajanta in the vicinity. A wonderful restaurant which no longer exists today. But it remained my favourite till it existed. This was my first of numerous visits to Ajanta that were to come in next five years

After ten days, Shaivalya left and Ankan arrived. Ankan was a young guy but a wonderful person to work with. He had just passed out of the UTI Institute of Capital markets (Now NISM) and had joined our department as management trainee in 2006. He was an assistant manager by now and was doing wonderful work for the department. As I and Ankan were closer in age, we would venture out in the evenings and take a walk around the Hotel. Ethiopia, for a long period of time, was a safe place to be and not like many African counterparts where you cannot move out after the dusk. We could walk around and spend time looking at this city.

It was during one such walk that we encountered the "university girl" scam. This is a very interesting scam that ran for many years in Ethiopia, especially in Addis Ababa. One day we were walking around the hotel, a well-behaved Ethiopian walked up to us and said "I have seen you in Ghion Hotel" He told he works in the hotel and now was going home for the day. Then he asked us "do you want to spend some good time" He had a wink in his eyes. He further said there is a party of university girls around here and if we want, we can join him. We had realised that this is something fishy and said no. He kept talking to us and to get rid of him I told him we work for Indian Army! Still he kept pushing to come with him. Eventually, he thought we were gay and that's why we're not coming with him. I was furious when he said this. I caught hold of his hand and told him he should come to our room. He was scared and ran away! It was hilarious. Many years later, I realised this is very common scam. Guys don't work at any hotel. They just guess about your hotel and target. They take the target to some deserted place and ask you to pay money.

One of the things that distinguished the upcoming ECX with MCX was the use of technology. MCX and Financial Technology was trying very hard to push their technology to be adopted by Ethiopia. However, the Ethiopian project team and more specifically Dr Eleni seemed to be convinced that the investment into technology does not need to be so high in the initial days. In hindsight I find this to be the right decision, as an alternative they had decided to run the Open Outcry model, which was phasing out in India, but was still used in many exchanges globally. One of the uniqueness of our training programs used to be the simulation exercise where we would simulate market conditions in an electronic trading environment and make people trade as if they're trading in real market. Like a real market, news would come and people have to react to that news and take trading decisions.

For this, a full-fledged simulation system, that was exact replica of the original trading system of MCX, was developed by Financial Technologies for the training department to use. However, since the ECX had decided to use an open outcry method, this simulation exercise could not be used. We had run a session when they were in India, but the Ethiopian team, when in India, insisted that there should be a simulation exercise for open outcry as well. Nobody in the department knew how to do it. We tried our best to push to them an online trading simulation, but they also wanted simulation for open outcry.

As the in charge of the training in India, I brought an innovation. During my days as a student and later on as head of the department for MFA course in Shri Vaishnav Institute of Management, I had organised a trading game called Bulls and Bears. This was trading game where people would come and trade in artificial trading pit. I immediately called up one of my very close friend Dr Niraj Vijayvergiya, who had mastered this game and had helped me in arranging for this game previously. He guided me to plan it correctly. Two of my students- Hitesh Sethia and Giridhari Kawadkar, were now working with me in MCX and had also played this game. Three of us chalked out a way to run a simulation game similar to the model that Ethiopia was planning to use. This became an instant hit and we replayed in Ethiopia as well. Ankan was very good with excels and he developed an excel sheet to record the trades and give out profits and losses. We rather successfully concluded our three-week stay with a simulation game being played in open outcry. This success of the open outcry-based simulation was to come back to challange me later.

As instructed by our management, we also had to run the online simulation, so that people can see the need for FT system. This needed an active support from our office in Mumbai, through the internet. We were to connect and play the online simulation game. Everything was tested by Shaivalya before he left. When we finally had to use it, we could not connect to the servers in Mumbai. Panicked, we called back to our colleagues in Mumbai, only to realise that MCX was under IT raid and all servers and computers what inaccessible for next few days. Faced this challenge, we somehow managed to run the simulation exercise using the backup server which was on and could be accessed. However, we both knew that this was not what we had planned.

I returned from Ethiopia on 7th of July 2007 after three weeks of stay in Ethiopia and those three weeks were life changing for me. My first visit to a foreign country finally came to an end but it was just a beginning....

CHAPTER TWO

FLIGHT TO ADDIS

In the first week of July 2007, I returned from Ethiopia and was very happy with what we had achieved there. A lot of accolades was flowing in from Ethiopia. A lot of people appreciated our effort in Ethiopia, and overall, it was a highly successful visit within the MCX. However, within the training department, the success of the visit was not as vigorously celebrated as I would have imagined. This was the time when the training department in MCX was getting broadly divided into two groups: the Mumbai team and the Indore team. This might sound funny, but that was the reality. After my recruitment into the training department, a few more Indore guys were recruited. At that time, the training department was headed by Mr. Saleem Andrews. Even later, more people were recruited from Indore. In total, five to six people from Indore, including myself, were part of the training department.

However, as the training department grew and Dr. Chiragra Chakrabarthy took over as the head of the department, the dynamic started to change. He started to recruit people identified by him, and a lot of his classmates and friends were recruited. This led to a division within the team between Indore and Mumbai. Also adding to the dynamics, Dr. Madhu Pawaskar, a very senior economist and a living legend of the commodity market who was also the mentor to Jignesh Shah, then MD of MCX, was overseeing the operations of the training department. He had his own idea of the future of the training department. He wanted it to be a research organization, while Dr. Chiragra was looking to make it a consulting firm. Due to the vision of Dr. Chiragra, consulting was becoming a major arm of the training department.

This led to a debate in the company about the role of the training department. The management was of the opinion that the training department should get involved in consulting, while many believed that, as it is a support function for the exchange, it should remain as such. The management of the exchange believed that it should eventually become an independent company, and hence, the consulting business should be seriously persuaded. Dr. Pawaskar, on the other hand, wanted it to be a research and publication entity, which led to a lot of planned publications. This led to a confused recruitment policy where senior people from consulting were recruited. At the same time, the whole editorial team was recruited. Interestingly, most of the recruitments were made at a higher level, whereas the old employees of the department ended up remaining junior. The team recruited eight to nine assistant vice presidents, whereas the old staff with similar experience remained below senior managers.

I have been outspoken and have said things in life that I could have avoided saying. But somehow, I end up speaking. I recall an incident in which I ended up mocking my boss Dr Chiragra over the Mumbai versus Indore debate. Though I thought I was saying it in a joking manner, I believe it left an impact on my then boss. While talking about my recent Indore visit, I told him that I had taken my daughter, who was about a year old then, to a market. There was a pony for kids to ride. When I showed her, she called it a donkey! He asked me, What do you mean? to which I replied, My daughter is a typical Mumbaiwali." He looked confused, and I created more damage by saying, ***Sir, Mumbai Walon ko Indore ka ghoda bhi gadha dikhta hai***! He laughed, but I know serious damage was done. Though, even after this, we maintained good relations, occasionally met, and even tried to work together until his unfortunate death in 2022. Still, I feel like that was one of the stupidest things I have done in my career.

There was a lot of distrust and corporate politics going on within the MCX training department. I remember once being sent to Indore without a proper briefing for a training program by one of the assistant vice presidents. He had also shared with me the agenda for the training program. Since I had travelled back from Jaipur the same morning, I had no time to prepare. I had to leave by evening and asked a colleague to copy the presentation on the laptop. When I reached Indore and got a chance to look at the agenda and the presentation, I tried to open the presentation. The presentation was password-protected, and I called up the colleague to share the password, only to be told that he had forgotten it. I was left with just two to three hours for the program and no presentation files with me. Somehow it was managed, and I started the session. A few minutes into the session, I realized that the agenda given to me and the other participants was entirely different. I understood it was a setup for me to fail. However, God has always been kind, and I navigated through that situation without much trouble.

The purpose of highlighting the issues is to give background on the second training program call from Ethiopia. A second training program was scheduled in Ethiopia, and this time, since the name was again suggested by Ethiopians, my boss had no second thought in sending me along with my colleague Venkat Giridhar. Venkat was an interesting character. He was a very capable and intelligent fellow in his work. He used to bring a lot of new ideas to the team. His understanding of the subject was really strong. But he was having challenges with people management skills within the department. When working with the team in the training department, it was not very easy for him. However, I still believe that he was a wonderful asset for the company.

For the second round of training, it was me and Venkat who were assigned to go to Ethiopia. The training program was for a duration of two weeks this time. This time it was comparatively easy for us as the place was known, the training schedule was well developed, and the flow was well developed. We reached Ethiopia on October 21, 2007 and stayed there for two weeks. The training program was arranged at a training facility established by the Red Cross. It was a well-designed centre with accommodations as well as training facilities on the same premises. The challenge this time was that there were two batches running simultaneously. I and Venkat had to come out of one session and go into another. This was far more exhausting than the earlier training. I and Venkat managed it successfully, with the cherry on top being our open outcry-based simulation.

One of the days, I guess the 26th of October, we had the reception, where the then state minister of agriculture, Yakob Yalla, also participated. We were introduced to him as the trainers from India. Dr Eleni said to him, introducing me, "You know, sir, we want to bring Bharat to Ethiopia" I was shocked to hear that statement, as prior to this, I never thought that this might be a possibility. However, trying not to look shocked, I immediately said, Sir, if you give me a chance, I'll be very happy". Dr Eleni said "I am taking you on record for saying this". I responded "You can". However, I thought it was just a casual way to show appreciation. But I was wrong.

Dr Eleni later told me to meet her before I left. She said "Please come and meet me before you go" Things were happening very fast, and I was not very sure how to go and meet her. We were in a facility that was all-inclusive. In two weeks, we had never been out. I was also worried about how Venkat would react to it. Finally, I decided to go and meet her on Saturday before leaving at night. I went to see Dr. Eleni without telling Venkat about my outing.

When I met Dr. Eleni, she told me that she had offered Dr Chiragra to loan me to the ECX Project for a year. She said, "You know, Bharat, I had requested Dr Chiragra to send you here for one year, and we will pay the consulting charges to MCX. But Dr Chiragra had refused, stating that there are a lot of things going on in India and he cannot send you for one full year." I sometimes wonder what would have happened had Dr Chiragra accepted the offer. Could I have achieved what I have in that case? I guess Dr Chiragra made a good decision on that.

She further said, "But I still want you here" She followed up with a straight question: "Would you like to come and work with us?" I was quite shocked and, honestly, not prepared for such an offer. I very politely told her that I would be happy to, but I would have to talk to my family and let you know. It will be only after I speak to them that I can decide. She said it's absolutely fine and told me to let her know when I make up my mind. She added that the project would love to have me in Ethiopia. That night, as we flew back to India, I could not sleep for a moment. The thought of going to Ethiopia to work with Dr. Eleni did seem like a distant possibility, but it is still something to consider at least.

Back at MCX, I had stopped enjoying the work as the work environment within the department had become very difficult. The power struggle between Dr. Pawaskar and Dr. Chiragra had ended in the separation of the teams. A lot of old colleagues had either moved out of the department or resigned. My mentor and colleague Shaivalya had also resigned, citing health issues, and by

December, the head of department, Dr. Chiragra, had also resigned. At this time, work was being done to separate the training department from MCX into a training and consulting company. I was not very sure that I would go to Ethiopia, but I was surely on the lookout for change.

I was more happy working with MCX as an institution than with a new group company of the Financial Technologies Group. The urge to stay in India's leading commodity exchange, the opportunity to move into operational roles, better financial prospects—all these factors were playing on my mind. In such a situation, Dr. Eleni made me an offer to come and work in Ethiopia. After returning from Ethiopia, I spent some days assessing it. Then I discussed it with my wife. As always, she said if you feel that is the right decision, you should decide to take it. She has been my strength and has always stood by me in challenging times. Our daughter was just two years old, and relocating was a very big decision. I spoke to my parents, who also supported it.

Now, with family backing the decision, I had more reasons to think about it seriously. I started evaluating the pros and cons of such a decision and honestly did not have much of an inclination to move to Ethiopia. I must admit that Ethiopia is not considered an immigration destination for Indians, at least by then. When talking about immigrating, people would look forward to going to either Europe or America. If not, then Southeast Asia at the minimum. But Africa was not a destination where people would migrate in search of better career prospects. The first person I discussed very openly and elaborately was Dr. Nitin Joshi. He was a big reason behind my decision, and as a result, he became a big reason for the success I had in my life

When I spoke to friends, a lot of people discouraged me, saying it's a third-world country and it will be a challenge to live there. Think about your daughter's education, health, and everything else. Someone even said, "I have heard there is famine in Ethiopia. How will you get food"? After fifteen years now, when I look back at it, it seems so hilarious. The basic question was, "Why do you want to leave such a wonderful job and go and settle down in such a poor country?" Most of these apprehensions were driven by ignorance about Africa. People highlighted issues like safety and security. However, Dr Nitin told me to base my decision on the experience I had, as I had spent some time in Ethiopia. I felt pretty confident and became more inclined to explore the options in Ethiopia. As I was in Indore for Diwali, I could discuss it with family and friends and make up my mind.

After Diwali, I wrote an email to my friends in Ethiopia and Dr. Eleni. She immediately responded back, saying that she would like me to join the team in Ethiopia. She detailed out the responsibility for me as head of the trading department and wanted me to help her set up the exchange trading system—at first the open outcry and later the electronic. I think the innovation of running an open-outcry simulation was a very important reason for her decision. She believed that I had very relevant experience from MCX, which could help me really add value to the team in Ethiopia. In her email, she indicated we should have a telephone call to discuss the relocation.

Honestly, I was not immediately prepared to respond. Though I had made up my mind, I was still not very sure that this could be decided so quickly, and I was still going back and forth on the idea.

I made up my mind in mid-December 2007 to explore and see what opportunities she was offering. After a lot of back and forth, I and Dr. Eleni were finally able to speak around Christmas, and she offered me a six-month job. The job offer was from the International Food Policy Research Institute (IFPRI), where the ECX Project was housed. I was offered a research assignment, but in practice, I was invited as head of the trading operations department. She also shared the financial benefit package, which I guess I should not disclose. The role, the opportunities, and the compensation package, even for six months, were exciting enough. I agreed to it, and finally, the New Year's Day of 2008 brought the much-awaited good news. In my inbox was the proposed agreement. I was to join on February 1, 2008.

I was very excited and started my final evaluations to accept or refuse the assignment. Moving out of India for six months was still a very brave decision. In hindsight, I believe that taking some brave decisions has made the difference in my life. However, it was the first time I was to make such a decision; I took another twenty days to tie up the loose ends. I finally resigned from MCX on January 21, 2008. Immediately, a lot of people, especially in the department, believed that this was my ploy to get a favourable appraisal and get better increments. By then, Dr. Chiragra had moved out, and Dr. Jinesh Panchali, a wonderful gentleman, had taken over as the head of the department. Dr. Jinesh was very different from Dr. Chiragra and had a very soft approach. He was bringing a more amicable environment to the department. He personally called me to ask the reason for my resignation. I had to remain very tight-lipped about my option in Ethiopia.

I had a standard answer for everyone: I was getting into the consulting business on my own and preferred working independently rather than working for any organization. The reason I gave, to a certain extent, was true, as my role with Ethiopia Project at the time was that of a consultant for six months, and after six months I had no guarantee of any job in Ethiopia. The usual HR practices of offering a higher salary and promotion were offered, but I had made up my mind. Though the uncertainty after six months was a spoiler, I finally made up my mind. I remember spending hours and hours with my friend Dr. Nitin Joshi, who was also in the process of moving to Welingkar Institute on Management. I remained tight-lipped on this, and even my protégés Hitesh Sethia and Giridhari Kawadkar did not know about it. Very honestly, I myself was not very sure about how long I would be in Ethiopia. I had decided to take the risk.

During my two and a half years with MCX, I spent a lot of weekends on training programs. This had led to a lot of accumulated compensatory leaves that I had not claimed. I was hopeful that MCX would adjust my accumulated leaves, which were sufficient in number to cover my notice period, and relieve me at the earliest. Dr. Eleni was pushing me to join IFPRI in Ethiopia by the first week of February. Finally, things worked out in my favour, and I was released from MCX duties on January 25, 2008. This was within four days of my resignation. As per the custom we had, a cake was to be brought to give a send-off from the department. It was only Hitesh and Giridhari who decided to bring the cake and give me a send-off. The formalities for the department were done quickly. Only Hitesh and Giridhari in the department were going to miss me, I guess. However, a lot of friends from other department of MCX, I still have a very strong bond.

Honestly speaking, on the last day of my work in MCX, I did not have a firm contract with IFPRI. Dr Eleni had indicated, however, that I have faith that the contract would be signed and executed soon. I had to do a lot of planning before I left, as I was leaving for six months. I was not sure when I would be able to visit India. I quickly became busy preparing for my travel. The first step was to secure a visa for travel. I got the invitation letter and had to go to Delhi to get the visa. During this time, another interesting incident happened. I had booked myself on a 6 a.m. flight from Mumbai to Delhi to get my visa. Traveling with all my documents in my bag, I was sitting in the airport waiting area to board my flight. Suddenly, I see my colleague Venkat Giridhar walk into the waiting area. I was stunned and started to think about what he was going to ask me. He saw me and came to greet me. Casually, he asked me where I was traveling. I told him that I was traveling to Delhi to meet someone and would be back in the evening.

We started to have a chat, and he started to explain to me how MCX is full of opportunities and how it is the wrong decision to resign from MCX. I could see genuine concern and advice coming from him. He made a valid point, stating that there is a new boss, the whole organization could be restructured, and because we have been doing so much international work, we will continue to travel across the world for our work. This is not the time to leave. In fact, in the coming months, he and my other colleagues did do some phenomenal work across the world. But, I was not convinced, as I had my plans and was looking forward to my visa. It was very cold in Delhi when I went to the Ethiopian Embassy in Chanakyapuri and submitted my documents for a visa. As all the documents were proper, the person in charge told me to come at 4 p.m. and collect the visa. I was waiting for my visa so that I could travel to Ethiopia and start a new life with new challenges. In the evening, I returned to Mumbai and had mixed emotions: sadness for leaving the family and excitement for working on an amazing project in Ethiopia.

Finally, on February 10th, at 5:50 AM, I departed for Ethiopia on an Ethiopian Airlines flight. This was to bring an entirely new dimension to my life. It was a flight that would lead me around the world. It was a Sunday, and when I landed in Ethiopia, my friend Solomon, who had been driving me around on my last two visits, was at the airport to receive me and take me to the hotel where I was accommodated. For those familiar with Addis, there is a beautiful apartment hotel called Bole Ambassador, just behind the Millennium Hall. This was where I spent my first ten days in Ethiopia. IFPRI, as a part of the package, had arranged for my accommodation for the first ten days. In those ten days,

I was to find out and find a house to stay in. With the help of some new friends in the ECX project team, I was able to zero in on an apartment opposite the iconic Sangam Restaurant in Addis Ababa. Addis Ababa did not have a lot of apartments, and people preferred Villas or bungalows instead of apartments. There were a few apartment buildings that were built by the government. The apartment I selected was on the 8th floor, though it was numbered seven, as the numbering started from the second floor, from where the residential apartment started. The ground floor and the first floor are for commercial outlets. I saw an elevator and asked the owner if I could use it. Mimi, the owner, said, "I don't know, as I have never used it". Later, I came to know that it was operated once, and at that time, people were stuck for a few hours. I decided to walk up and down the eight floors every day.

Apart from the elevator, the bigger challenge in the apartment was the dogs. After 7 p.m., when it started to be dark, the ground and the first floor of the apartment building became homes for a lot of stray dogs. Being scared of dogs, passing them while climbing up the stairs was absolutely impossible. So, I had to ensure that I reached my apartment before 6 p.m. in the evening. If not, I had to pay the guard ten birr to take the dogs away for a walk. These dogs started to disappear after a Chinese restaurant was opened in the vicinity. They probably did not like the smell.

For the first ten days, Solomon used to pick me up in the morning and drop me off at the hotel in the evening. After the days, I had to either take a taxi or the minibus to the office. The office was located in an old building, which was termed Buna-Na-Shay. Buna, in Amharic, means coffee, and Shay means tea. It was the building managed and controlled by the coffee and tea authority in Ethiopia. I would get a minibus to go to the office just outside my apartment, and the minibus would drop me just outside my office. Quickly, I adjusted to the crammed-up minibus and started to feel comfortable in that mode. The first word I learned in Ethiopia was VORACHAALE, which meant I wanted to get down. This is what you had to say when the minibus reached your destination.

Another interesting revelation I had after reaching Ethiopia was on my second day of arrival. I arrived on a Sunday and spent most of the day resting. On Monday, I joined the office. In the evening, as I realized that I needed some Ethiopian Birr for my expenses, I requested Solomon to take me to a bank. I knew the banks worked until 3:30 in the afternoon. When I reached one of the banks, it was 3:35 p.m. . I told them that I wanted to change some currency. The lady on the counter said she would have helped me, but the bank is now closed. I asked her what time it will open. She looked at the watch and said 3:30. I thought she was telling me the closing time. I asked again, "Tomorrow morning, what time will it open?" She again said 3:30. Now I changed my question and asked, "When does it close?" She answered at 9:30. I thought she had messed up the opening and closing timings and the bank would open at 9:30. As I came back to the car, Solomon asked me if I was able to get the change. I told him the bank had closed. He looked at the watch and said yes, it's 9:30, so it's closed now. I was super confused, as Solomon was also talking about the 9:30 time! I asked him, How is 9:30? It is 3:30, right?" He revealed to me that it is 3:30 p.m. as per European timing but 9:30 as per Ethiopian timing.

I didn't understand what he meant. I asked him again, What is the difference between European time and Ethiopian time? He then told me that 3:30 p.m. in European time is referred to as 9:30 a.m. in Ethiopia. I was still confused and reserved the clarification for my old friend Ben. The next day, when I met Ben and asked him about this confusion, he laughed it out and said, "Oh, so you have not understood the difference between the Ethiopian and the European timings." I said, "No, this is the first time I am coming across such a thing. He explained to me that Ethiopian days start at sunrise , at 6 a.m. . So 6 a.m. is considered zero, and going from there, the count of one, two, and three goes on, which means 7 a.m. is 1 a.m. in Ethiopia, and that way, 9:30 a.m. in European time is 3:30in Ethiopian time. This was an interesting revelation for me, and I started to understand the difference between European and Ethiopian time. So next time if you are in Ethiopia and somebody invites you for lunch and gives you a time of 6:30 a.m., don't be confused; that's the lunch time of 12:30 p.m. as per European time.

Navigating through this new time challenge, I was sucked into the work almost immediately. The project team had set itself a target to launch the exchange by April 2008. Though it was an ambitious target, exciting times were in store for me. On the second day of my work in Ethiopia, initial technology consultant Jawad Ali had scheduled a presentation on the system overview. I was put to work immediately, but what helped me most from that presentation session was that everyone learned the difference between Bharat and Baaraat. Still, many people in Africa and the US pronounce my name as Baaraat. Jawad was kind enough to tell them "Bharat is my name, and Baaraat is a wedding procession". From that day on, no one called me Baaraat. At least no one who was present there.

CHAPTER THREE

ETHIOPIA: CRADLE OF MANKIND

When we say Africa, when we say India, most people think it to be South Africa. Very rarely do people realize that Africa is a continent, not a country, that is made up of 54 different countries. However, in India, Africa is synonymous with South Africa. Most people know Kenya due to their semi-final outing against India in the 2003 Cricket World Cup and the Masai Mara game reserve. When you say Ethiopia, not many people in India know where it is. Some people know it due to the famine that hit Ethiopia in the 1980s. Other people, apart from those who have explored Africa, rarely know that a country named Ethiopia exists. With so much media around, things are changing. Back in 2007-2008, when I was planning to relocate to Ethiopia, most people in India felt it was a disease-ridden, barbaric land. However, it is important to put on record that Ethiopia is such a wonderful nation. As I arrived in Ethiopia, I started to know a lot more about the country that kept fascinating me.

Ethiopia is also one of the most populous countries in Africa and, by far, the most populous country in East Africa. The current population of Ethiopia is estimated to be 120 million, second only to Nigeria in the African context. When I moved to Ethiopia in 2008, the country's population was roughly 80 million people. In those times also, it was still a large number considering the population of various other African countries. However, in spite of the huge population dividend, it was a county with the lowest life expectancy and poor infrastructure. What Ethiopia is today is very different from what it was in 2008.

The capital city of Ethiopia is Addis Ababa. This city itself is home to about 5.4 million people. As my flight descended into Addis on February 10, 2008, I could see lush green surroundings around Addis Ababa. This city, founded in the 19th century by Emperor Menelik, seems like a gateway to another world for everyone. For the rural masses of Ethiopia, it is a city of dreams, a city whose streets are paved in gold. At the same time, for someone like me, a foreigner, it appears to be the gateway to an ancient and mystical world.

My first experience of Addis Ababa in my past visits was like any other city in the developing world. It does appear to be a big, dusty, overcrowded city at first sight, but very few people in India know that the same Addis Ababa is the diplomatic capital of Africa. Addis Ababa is home to the African Union. The African Union is the joint body of 54 African countries. Addis also hosts the headquarters of the United Nations Economic Commission for Africa. The UN System in Ethiopia is one of the largest in the world and covers both development and humanitarian assistance. The UN Country Team (UNCT) in Ethiopia is composed of representatives of twenty eight UN funds, programs, and specialized agencies. Addis Ababa is home to the third-largest United Nations population and has representation from nearly every foreign embassy from around the world. Besides, there was a substantial presence of international NGOs in Addis as well. Some of the very good friends that I have today I met in Addis as they worked either for these International NGOs, the UN agencies, or even the Indian Embassy.

Addis Ababa is located at a height of 2355 m. It is the third-highest capital city in the world and the highest in Africa. It draws its name from the Amharic word for new flower. However, after I arrived in Addis, I experienced some shortness of breath, fatigue, nausea, headaches, and an inability to sleep within the first few days of arriving. I thought it was due to the physical and mental overload of the past month. But later, I realized this is part of the altitude sickness that even the fittest may experience in Addis. Over the first month, after having a natural cardio of climbing eight floors up and down every day in Addis Ababa, the challenges of the altitude probably made my lungs quite powerful!

One of the landmark institutions in Addis Ababa is the African Union. It is Emperor Haile Selassie 1 who is credited with being a strong force behind the establishment of the African Union. He promoted the concept of pan-Africanism, a movement that eventually led to the birth of the African Union. Though the African Union was formally established in 2002, in order to promote unity and solidarity among African states, spur economic development, and promote international cooperation, its predecessor was the Organization of African Unity (OAU). This organization was formed in 1963, with Emperor Haile Selassie 1as the first chairperson.

Ethiopia has the most UNESCO World Heritage Sites in Africa. The nine UNESCO sites in Ethiopia are Aksum, Fasil Ghebbi, Harar Jugol, Konso Cultural Landscape (which was not registered as a UNSESCO site in 2008), Lower Valley of the Awash, Lower Valley of the Omo, The Rock-Hewn Churches of Lalibela, and Tiya. However, the biggest regret I have is that I was not able to visit them during my stay in Ethiopia. I will probably visit once just to see these sites. One day.

Whenever we talk about Africa, invariably, the scramble for Africa, the so-called partition of Africa, or the conquest of Africa come up. This refers to the invasion of European powers and their colonization of Africa in the late 1800s and early 1900s. This divided the African continent into the Anglophonic (primarily east Africa, English-speaking, ruled by the British) and Francophonic (primarily west Africa, French-speaking, primarily ruled by France, some by Belgium). Some territories were also ruled by Germany and Portugal. However, in this conquest, Ethiopia was an exception. Ethiopia remained independent and sovereign throughout this period. It has never been colonized throughout the so-called scramble. No colonial power from the west has ever been able to occupy or colonize Ethiopia. This fact is very proudly told to you by locals when you meet them. After I spent a few days in Ethiopia, I started to hear people very proudly say that in the past five thousand years, no European has ever ruled Ethiopia. It's not that efforts were not made by the European powers to conquer Ethiopia. Ethiopia has been at war with Italian forces twice. However, both times, they defeated the Italian forces and failed in their efforts to colonize Ethiopia. Surely a fact to be proud of.

As I settled down in Addis after my arrival in February, I was told that on March 2, there would be a public holiday. I asked a friend, who told me it was Adwa Victory Day. Curious about it, I asked a friend to tell me more about it. He told me the story of the Battle of Adwa. It was between 1895 and 1896 that the first Italian-Ethiopian war was fought. In 1889, the Italian forces in Eretria signed a treaty (the Treaty of Wuchale) with King Menelik II. The Italians claimed that this treaty turned Ethiopia into an Italian Protectorate. However, in a full-scale war, Italian troops from Eritrea attacked Ethiopia. Initially, they met with some success, until Ethiopian troops led by king Menelik II counter-attacked their position and defeated them in the small town of Adwa to force them to surrender.

The battle of Adwa on March 1, 1896, resulted in a stunning victory for Ethiopia but a disaster for Italy. It was a critical blow that forced them to withdraw to Eritrea. This war ended with the Treaty of Addis Ababa and became the foremost symbol of pan-Africanism. This astounding victory is still celebrated with pride in Ethiopia. The result of the victory was that Ethiopia remained independent until 1936. It was in 1936 that the Italian forces launched the second attack on Ethiopia, and were successful in occupying the country for six years until 1941. Ethiopian forces fought back and finally regained control. As I asked a friend about the second Italy-Ethiopia war, he said, You know, we let them build railways and other infrastructure and then kicked them out. Ethiopia was one of the members of the League of Nations established in 1920, which condemned the Italian invasion in 1935; however, they could not impose any serious economic sanctions on Italy.

As an Indian, I realized soon that the response was very different. It is important to note that Indians in Ethiopia have more respect and connections than in other East African countries. It is sometimes easier to be an Indian in Ethiopia than an European. Ethiopian schools have for more than hundred years now had Indian teachers, and a lot of Ethiopians have studied at various universities in India. This makes them respectful towards Indians. Invariably, anyone you meet will tell you "My teacher was an Indian". Not only the teachers, but the soft power of India—Bollywood—also has a very strong impact on Ethiopians. They know Amitabh Bachhan, Shakhrukh Khan, Hritik Roshan, and, of course, Bhaijaan-Salmaan Khan.

One thing I noticed immediately after my arrival was the way the Ethiopians greet each other. They will shake hands and slightly knock their shoulders together, a gesture known as the "fighters' salute". I quickly learned the way and still greet my Ethiopian friends that way. They are especially proud of their military history. Very few know that the first female pilot to shoot down an enemy fighter jet in combat was an Ethiopian. A female Ethiopian captain, Aster Tolossa, became the first female fighter pilot to shoot down an enemy aircraft in the history of Aerial warfare in the year 2000, when she shot down an enemy plane near Asmara, Eritrea, in the Eritrean airspace.

I am a history buff, and I used to spend a lot of time talking to people about the history of Ethiopia. I realized that the history of Ethiopia is rich, including the history of rulers, the emperors and queens. The last ruler of Ethiopia was Haile Selassie 1. The Ethiopian emperors are considered the descendants of King Solomon and Makeda, the Queen of Sheba. As per the biblical references, The queen of Sheba visited King Solomon with an abundance of gold, precious stones, and spice. She asked difficult questions to Solomon, who answered them. It is believed that the queen of Sheba was the queen of Abyssinian land, which is Ethiopia in present-day Ethiopia. Certainly, it is a civilization with a lot of history and references.

I have already spoken about the confusion of Ethiopian time. The Ethiopians measure their time based on sunrise to sunset, and 6:00 is considered sunrise. So the clock starts at 6:00 a.m. After a few days of moving into the apartment, I developed confusion. There used to be a travel agent on the ground floor of the apartment who had a permanent sign: **Ethiopia, a country with 13 months of sunshine**. I never understood if it was a mistake or if the Ethiopian calendar really has thirteen months. I knew that different cultures in the world, like those in India and Nepal, have their own calendars. But all the calendars have twelve months.

Ben used to be my guide whenever I had any such confusion. He explained the concept. Most of the world, including India, which has its own calendar, now prefers to follow the Gregorian calendar. This calendar is divided into twelve months. However, Ethiopia still follows its traditional calendar. The traditional Ethiopian calendar has more than twelve months. The Ethiopian calendar has twelve months of thirty days and one month of five to six days, making a total of three hundred and sixty five days. This calendar changes the year on September eleven every year. So unlike the rest of the world, Ethiopia does not have celebrations on December thirty first at midnight for the new year, but has those celebrations three months in advance on September eleventh. I realized that on December thirty first, 2008, when no new year's parties (except the private ones) were planned and it was a common night in Ethiopia,

The Ethiopian calendar is called the Ge'ez calendar. This calendar is based on the Coptic Calendar. Not only in terms of months, this calendar also has a different year system. The Ethiopian calendar is seven to eight years behind the Gregorian calendar. This is because of the alternate calculation in determining the date of the annunciation of the birth of Jesus; the calendar has a different date. In Ethiopia, it is the year 2015, when the world has moved into 2023. This reminds me of a very interesting story that a friend of mine encountered. This friend of mine was working for an international company based in Europe. No one in the head office was aware of the Ethiopian calendar. Before I get into this story, it's important to learn another unique thing about Ethiopia. Ethiopia has its own language, called Amharic. This language has its own script. Every African country has its own language, but the script is not common. Most African languages are written in English. But Ethiopia is one of the very few countries globally that has its own language and script.

Most of the official communication in Ethiopia is in Amharic. Though there are more than eighty different languages spoken in Ethiopia, with more than two hundred types of dialects and variations, Amharic is the most common language. Apart from Amharic, Oromo, Somali, and Tigrinya are other languages that are spoken in Ethiopia. As I mentioned earlier, the city name Addis Ababa means new flower in Amharic. Official documents are made in Amharic, and there are official government translators who would translate them to English if required. Ethiopians are very proud of their language, culture, and history, and as a result, they do not feel it is mandatory to use English as an official language. As Ethiopia has never been colonized, the use of English and the propagation of English have only occurred in recent years. Otherwise, English speaking is not a skill as developed as you would find in countries like Kenya or Ghana.

So, coming back to my friend's story, this friend of mine worked for an international company based in Europe, and the company had opened a representative office in Ethiopia. As per the regulation, every year the company had to pay the fees and get the license renewed. This was the first renewal for the company. The company made a transfer to the account for him to pay the fees and other charges for the office. He made all the payments and sent the receipts back to the company head office in Europe for confirmation of expenses. This was his first year in Ethiopia, when he got the license and everything renewed. The license was issued in Amharic as per the policy. There was an English translation of the same provided, but the date was as per the Ethiopian calendar. This was the year 2009, and the receipt issued and the license approved carried the date of 2001. My friend did not realize this and sent it to the audit team in Europe, only to have the audit team raise a query. The audit team objected that he had submitted the wrong documents, and these documents are eight years old. My friend, realizing the problem, tried to convince the auditors about the calendar in Ethiopia, and the European office, being European, wanted the documents to be issued in English. When my friend inquired with the office, he was told point blank that in Ethiopia, the Ethiopian calendar is what we use. My friend was going through this confusion for days. The audit office was not ready to accept the documents and threatened to deduct money from his salary! One evening he met me, and I asked him about his confusion. He told the whole story. First I laughed, but then quickly I advised him to go and get the translation done again, and while the translation is done, he should request the translator to translate the date also. This solution worked, and the English translation certified by the government agency now included a European date of 2009. So when you are in Ethiopia, the time, the month, and the Year all have different meanings, so you have to be very particular about asking if it is the European or the Ethiopian day, time, or year.

While in Ethiopia, I used to see a lot of posters of Bob Marley with his Jamaican cap. Many people may know Bob Marley. Those who know him also know the Rastafarian movement. The Rastafarian movement was religious as well as social. Many people believe that the Rastafarian movement originated in Jamaica. Though the Rastafarian movement evolved in Jamaica, its spiritual roots are in Ethiopia. If you see the posters of Bob Marley, the Rastafarian movement, and the Ethiopian national flag, you will see the similarity. In Amharic, Ras is the title similar to chief, and Tafari is the name of Emperor Haile Selassie 1. The rastafarian movement considers Emperor Haile Selassie 1 the incarnation of Jah, which is the shortened version of Jehovah, whom Rastas believe is their god. Jehovah finds reference in the old testament and is used as the name for God. Right from its emergence, the Rastafarian movement was linked to Haile Selassie 1. A lot of Rastas believe that Haile Selassie was the incarnation of Jesus.

On April 21, 1966, Haile Selassie visited Jamaica. As his plane landed at the Jamaica airport, about hundred thousand Rastafari from all over Jamaica came to the airport. They surrounded Haile Selassie's plane on the tarmac. Haile Selassie emerged from the plane on the steps and waved at them. Many claim that they saw Haile Selassie with tears in his eyes. Some Rastafari claimed that they had seen the stigma marks on his hand, which were similar to those of Jesus after crucification. As the crowd was swelling, Haile Selassie could not get out of the plane and went inside. The Jamaican authorities requested that the leader of the Rastafari to come and help the emperor disembark. The leader went inside the plane and, after speaking to Haile Selassie , came down and told his colleagues that the emperor had told them to be calm and that he would be with them soon. Soon Haile Selassie , escorted by the Rasta leader, stepped down and surprisingly refused to walk on the red carpet. He rather preferred to walk on the ground, which Rastafari later claimed he did so as to make contact with the soil. Even today, Rastafari celebrate the day of April 21 as Groundation Day, when their God dissented on the Jamaican land.

Ethiopia, by far, is a very old civilization. It is the cradle of mankind. In 1972, Donald Johanson, Maurice Taieb, Yves Coppens, and Tom Gray discovered Lucy, or Dinkinesh in Amharic, a 3.2 million-year-old skeleton as a collection of several hundred pieces of fossilized bone representing forty percent of a female hominid. It was then the oldest human remains found ever. For six years together, Lucy went on a worldwide tour and enjoyed widespread fame. Lucy was discovered in the Danakil Depression in the Afar region. The Danakil Depression is one of the world's hottest and lowest spots. It is hundred meters below sea level.

Soon, Lucy's predecessor, Ardi, was also discovered in the same area of Afar. Ardi was one million years older than Lucy and arguably became the oldest found hominid by now. It is not surprising that Ethiopia is called the "Cradle of Mankind." Even in their relative modern history, you find flourishing civilization in Axum

City in north Ethiopia. Axum is known for its relics of the ancient kingdom. It is believed to be the final resting place of the Arc of Covenant, which contained the ten commandments God gave to Moses. Not only this, Ethiopia also has Lake Tana, the birthplace of the longest river in the world, the Blue Nile. The Blue Nile originates from Ethiopia, and the White Nile originates from Lake Victoria. Both of them merge in Sudan and finally flow into Egypt.

Somewhere in 2009, Ethiopia decided to build a dam on the Blue Nile and named it the Grand Ethiopian Renaissance Dam. It was a megaproject that would generate sufficient electricity for Ethiopia to consume and sell the remainder to its neighbours. A very ambitious project was conceived under the leadership of then Prime Minister Meles Zenawi. However, Egypt had objections to the building of this dam. Ethiopia and Egypt have a historical relationship. Between 1874 and 1876, Ethiopia and Egypt locked horns in a war that resulted in an unequivocal victory for Ethiopia. This is known as the Battle of Gura. Ethiopians had ensured that their sovereignty remained intact with a victory in this war.

When, in 2011, the dispute between Egypt and Ethiopia emerged, the Ethiopian Prime Minister was very quick to issue a threat, saying that in the last war only one Egyptian remained alive to tell the story, and if there is a war again, no one will remain alive. Egypt was successful in convincing the United States, which had so long been an Ethiopian ally. The US "persuades" the World Bank to stop funding for this Dam. The funding for the Ethiopian Renaissance Dam was stopped. However,

Ethiopians, being the fighters they are, did not give up, and it was decided that every person in Ethiopia would contribute one month's salary towards the construction of the dam. Huge donations poured in from different Ethiopian public and private entities for the construction of the dam. Finally, Ethiopians were able to negotiate with the Chinese to support the dam's construction. It was a way of claiming victory for Prime Minister Meles Zenawi.

I spoke about the challenges in Addis due to altitude. This is a blessing for Ethiopia in the field of sports. Ethiopia has emerged in the international sporting arena since the 1960 Rome Olympics. It was in 1960 that Abebe Bikila became the first black African to win gold at the Olympics. Abebe was selected at the last minute as one of his teammates had a broken foot. Abebe ran barefoot in the marathon and was able to beat Moroccan runner Ben Abdesselam by 25 seconds. As this was the Rome Olympics, the newspaper in Ethiopia commented that it took an entire Italian army to conquer Ethiopia, whereas a single Ethiopian has conquered Rome. He won gold in the Tokyo Olympics as well, where he set the world record and became the first ever Olympic marathon runner to win gold twice. Marathon running is something that comes very naturally to Ethiopians. This gives Ethiopia a strong history of Marathon runners. The latest being Haile Gebre-Selassie. He has also won two Olympic gold medals in 1996 and 2000 in 10,000 meters and four world championship titles in the same event.

When it comes to food, Ethiopians love their raw meat. However, contrary to common belief, Ethiopians have a very strong taste for vegetarian food as well.

Ethiopian cuisine, by far, is more tasty, healthier, and diverse as compared to any other African traditional food. Most Ethiopians follow orthodox christianity, which prohibits eating any animal products on Wednesdays and Fridays. So, two days a week, Ethiopians turn vegetarian and have various vegetarian choices in their food. During the lint, Ethiopians observe a forty-day fast, during which they do not eat any sort of animal product. Any traditional Ethiopian restaurant would have various spicy vegan stews on their menu, which makes the lives of vegetarians much easier in Ethiopia. However, when you tell an Ethiopian that you do not eat meat, as an Indian, you mean you do not eat fish as well. Whereas in Ethiopia, fish is something you can eat if you are a vegetarian, but what you can't eat is milk or butter. The modern concept of vegan food is part of daily life in Ethiopia. On other days, Ethiopians eat Kitfo, which is raw minced meat consumed without cooking.

It is commonly believed in India that Africans can even eat human meat. This got more prominence after Idi Amin. However, I have never seen any such thing in Africa, but the stories continue. I remember a story about a very good friend of mine on a similar issue. He was working for Red Cross International in the conflict prevention area. Their role was to work closely with the tribal in interior Ethiopia and ensure that the tribal and modern societies don't come into conflict. The work also involved slowly making the tribe realize and adopt certain modern ways of life, which will help them improve their status. During one such interaction, he, who was a very lean, thin, short guy, along with a German colleague, travelled to a remote location in Southern Ethiopia. The

Germans were tall, well-built Europeans, and they were accompanied by their driver, who was known to the local tribes. The local tribe chief, after meeting them, said something to the driver, and the driver burst out laughing. Just to connect with the tribal chief, my friend and his German colleague inquired what the matter was. Both the driver and the chief avoided speaking about the matter, but the German colleague kept insisting. Finally, the driver explained to him what the tribal chief had said. He told that the tribal chief has requested him that "if this German dies in Ethiopia, please give us his body. He seems to be very tasty!" This tribe, at one point, used to eat human meat but has given up now. However, occasionally they were not averse to having one, as the German believed.

Ethiopia is a very old country and has references in both the Bible and the Quran. Ethiopia appears forty five times in the King James version of the Bible. It talks about the Queen of Sheba, who visited King Solomon. Ethiopia is also mentioned in the Quran. When Muhammad saw the persecution to which his followers were subjected in Mecca, he allegedly told them to find a safe haven in Abyssinia in northern Ethiopia, where they would find the king who does no wrong. Even in India, we find references to Ethiopian fighters. Very regularly in India, we use the word "Habshi" without realizing that Habshi originates from the word Habeshi, which was a reference to Ethiopians. The Siddi community, which might find reference in text pertaining to Chhatrapati Shivaji Maharaj's time, like Siddi Johar of the Murud Janjira Fort, are Ethiopians. They originated in Ethiopia and, through the slave trade route, went to Arabs and eventually to Mughals before coming to India. Today, there are also communities living in Telangana and Gujarat that have a physical appearance similar to Ethiopians but have been here for generations. I did not realize that Ethiopia was such a wonderful land with an old civilization before I reached it. The more I came to know about Ethiopia, the more I started to fall in love with this country.

In 2008, when I moved to Ethiopia, it was a time when Ethiopia was being rebuilt. In 1991, Ethiopia came out of a bloody civil war, after which the military junta called the Dergu was overthrown and replaced by a more democratically elected government. Ethiopian Prime Minister Meles Zenawi was a legendary leader and had very strong political acumen. The civil war from 1974 until 1991 was one of the darkest phases of Ethiopian history, where Ethiopia lost a lot of talent and growth opportunities due to the oppressive rule of Mengistu Haile Mariam. However, leaving that behind, Ethiopia, in 2008, was slowly becoming a reference point in Africa.

CHAPTER FOUR

NEED OF A COMMODITY EXCHANGE IN ETHIOPIA

When I decided to go to Ethiopia, one of the biggest worries that my friends in India had was about the availability of food in Ethiopia. The memories of the 1980 famine that affected Ethiopia were still very fresh in the minds of a lot of people in India that I interacted with. However, a lot of change had happened since then, and Ethiopia was moving towards becoming a developing nation by then. Looking into the history of the famine that hit Ethiopia between 1983 and 1985, we find that it was one of the worst famines to hit the Ethiopian people. Though, in the past, Ethiopia had faced draughts and famines, this was by far the most devastating one. It is estimated that around seven to eight million people were affected by the famine. This famine was not only a natural calamity but also the result of multiple factors.

The United Nations attributed a total of one million people as dead due to the famine and more than 2.5 million people as displaced out of the total population of 35–40 million. However, these figures are strongly contested, and it is realistically estimated that more or less three hundred to four hundred thousand people died in the famine. The important question is, could this famine be avoided? Well, there were multiple factors that resulted in this famine and made it a bigger catastrophe than it should have been. Nature had a role to play, but it was not entirely responsible. The major impact of the famine was in areas of Wollo, Tigery, and Eritrea. These areas had very difficult terrain and limited road and rail transport networks. Also, most of these areas were affected by the civil war. Ethiopia was inundated with a civil war between the Dergu, the ruinous military junta, and the rebels. This war was making it more difficult for aid agencies to reach out to the Ethiopian people with humanitarian aid. It is often said that the man-made factors triggered by war, like a lack of safe passages, fragile socio-economic conditions, and large-scale displacement, very quickly and severely converted a natural draught into a devastating famine.

Like any other sub-Saharan African country, Ethiopia also had its grain trade dominated by the marketing corporations that were set up in the late 1970s. Ethiopia, being a communist country in that period, had a very tightly controlled food distribution system, grain prices, and trade through a network of government agencies and enterprises. In 1975, the ruling party, under the leadership of Mengistu Haile Mariam, brought land reforms, transferred ownership of all land to the state, and provided allotments of no more than ten hectares to individual peasants who farmed the land themselves. Their communist ideology led the government to force the farmers to deliver grain at below-market prices, a measure that pushed the farmers into poverty and forced them to shun production in some cases. The government did not do anything to promote production. In that backdrop, when the drought intensified in 1984, the drought quickly transformed into a catastrophic famine. The government's control in those times further limited the options that farmers had been using previously to respond to shortfalls. There were more socio-political issues that I would restrict myself from discussing here.

As Ethiopia came out of the civil war in 1991, a lot of reforms were introduced, including the opening up of markets. By this time, the World Bank had started to dismantle the centralized marketing board system that led to government-controlled grain markets and had started to champion the free market concept. The World Bank and other donor agencies were hellbent on dismantling the central marketing board structures as a part of the economic liberalization movement.

One of the commodity sector institutions that gained prominence in the wake of the economic liberalization effort was the commodity exchange. The concept of commodity exchange was introduced by Dr Eleni in Ethiopia. Since 2002, when she was conducting research on Ethiopian market structures, she has kept advocating at different policy levels about the need to reform the marketing system in Ethiopia. Later, in 2005, Dr Eleni and Ian Goggin wrote a paper titled "Does Ethiopia need a commodity exchange". After this paper was published and discussed at the government level, Dr Eleni became the champion of commodity exchange in Ethiopia, though the initial paper was written by Dr Eleni with the help of Ian Goggin. Ian was already a practitioner in commodity exchanges and had set up commodity exchanges in Zimbabwe and Malawi. In this paper, the detailed technical knowledge about commodity exchange was contributed by Ian, whereas Dr Eleni brought in a deep understanding of the Ethiopian grain market. This knowledge she had gained over the years through numerous research projects in the Ethiopian grain market This paper actually highlighted the problems Ethiopia has and how these problems, which, in my opinion, are common to any underdeveloped agriculture-based economy, have contributed to the food insecurity that Ethiopia was facing.

Ethiopia was a large country with very minimal infrastructure for grain trade. In Ethiopia, the grain trade was dominated by small farmers and traders (aggregators), who were trading with very limited locally known counterparties. They would buy small quantities of grain from the farmer, aggregate it, and send it to players in their known vicinity. The trade was limited to a known group of family and friends and would be very local geographically.

Dr Eleni and Goggin, through their paper, suggested that the commodity exchange is the ideal solution for Ethiopia to have. By then, the commodity exchange concept was limited to the western world, with some asian countries adopting the commodity exchange system. However, almost all the commodity exchanges in the world were derivative exchanges, whereas Ethiopia was planning to introduce a spot exchange. This, in itself, was a unique feature, and if done correctly, it can have a long-lasting impact on the approach of Ethiopian agriculture and agricultural trade. Needless to say, the objective was to ensure food security and restructure the trade systems in Ethiopia. Through her continuous efforts since 2002, Dr. Eleni was able to convince the policymakers, and more importantly, win over the prime minister and the deputy prime minister to look into alternate mechanisms for developing the markets.

2002 was a year when Ethiopia was again facing a food crisis, and the then policymakers were desperate to find long-term solutions. Dr. Eleni, in her publication "A Market for Abdu," discusses how, in 2002, the food crisis followed years of bumper harvest. As a result of such a bumper harvest in the past two years, the prices of grain in Ethiopia were depressed, meaning that the farmers were not getting remunerative prices to take care of the basic costs of production. Due to this, in 2002, because of the shortage of inputs resulting from the inability of the farmers, the overall productivity went down, and Ethiopia fell short of its food production. Dr. Eleni suggested, as that publication highlights, how the overproduction has resulted in a problem for the farmer and for the overall food balance sheet of the country.

When you look at Ethiopia, you realize that the major problem there is common to a lot of agri-dependent developing countries, even India. In spite of India's phenomenal success through its green revolution, the markets have always been an area of concern for the agriculture sector. It still remains so. Though somehow India has been able to structure the agriculture trade, it is far from an ideal situation. In Ethiopia also, the situation of the agriculture markets was not good, and the markets were riddled with a number of inefficiencies. One such inefficiency was contract enforcement. Further, most of these inefficient markets, warehousing, and storage are absent, and the farmers and traders have no way to carry forward the grain as they wait for better prices. Most of the farmers and small village traders are forced to take their produce to the market and then sell it at whatever price they can.

In Ethiopia, as pointed out by Dr. Eleni in her paper, one of the major challenges of the market was trust. People were forced to trade between themselves, between whom they knew and with whom they had some prior connections. Beyond their known circle, they would not be trading, as they could not trust each other in the trade. I always believe that for a trade to happen, trust is paramount. If you develop trust, trade will happen. The reason this lack of trust came up was due to the fact that there used to be a lot of contract defaults. Prices would be agreed, but when the traders or the farmers transported the produce to the buyers, they refused to pay the price, and as a result, the Farmer or the Trader was left hanging.

Dr. Eleni pointed out a case that she learned about during her study of the Ethiopian markets. A trader, in search of better prices, invested in transporting the grain from one region in Ethiopia to another. It was only to find that when he reached the buyer's location with his grains, the buyer was no longer interested in honouring the contract that he had promised. This loss of trust ensured that the trader on the losing end would not, in any way, trade outside the known family and friends circle in the future. In most of the sub-Saharan agricultural markets, contract defaults are rampant and are one of the major reasons for unproductive trade in agricultural commodities.

This factor of trading only within their known circle creates further fragmentation in the market. One of the reasons that I get reminded of Ethiopia is the similar situation in Bengal, India during the Bengal famine. It was the inability of the market to transport grain from the surplus areas to the deficit areas. This is the classic case of a fragmented market in Ethiopia. southern Ethiopia had a reasonable amount of production that could sustain and, to a certain extent, reduce the impact of the drought in the northern areas. But the traders in the southern area had no mechanism for selling product in the northern area, which meant that the traders in the southern area suffered due to excess production and the people in the northern area suffered due to the non-availability of food. This fragmentation of the markets is one of the root causes of poor sector performance in the agriculture markets in most agriculture-dominated developing countries.

Adding to the worries are the transportation costs and the infrastructure of roads and railways. This is where India has an edge over many other countries, as in India we have a reasonably developed railway network, which could be leveraged to transport the grain from surplus areas to deficit areas. In Ethiopia, the market network was absent, and the movement of grain from one region to another was very expensive, to the tune of making it unviable to transport. The transport cost in Ethiopia, even in 2008, when I arrived, was exorbitantly high, which meant that the grain trade was costly, putting the overall cost of food on a higher level. Most sub-Saharan African countries have poor rail and road networks, and the availability of fuel also puts a challenge on transportation costs. When I was in Ethiopia, working on the exchange, I realized that big transport vehicles were owned by politically influential people, who ensured that the cost of transportation remained well above average. Their profits and the higher costs, however, meant that the markets became unviable and remained fragmented because of the higher transportation costs.

It's not only the cost of transport and default that the farmers face. One of the most common challenges that even today's farmers in India face is the quality of the assessment. Very rarely, the farmer is paid sufficiently for the quality of the grain. The quality of the offered grain is very subjectively decided throughout the world. In such markets, I have seen that it is the visual inspection and the subjective opinion of the buyer that define the quality. There are no benchmarks against which a product can be objectively evaluated and decided upon for its quality, As no premium is paid to the farmer for quality. The farmers also tend to be careless about handling and transportation, causing further losses in the process. This was also very prominent in Ethiopia.

I must recall here that when we were done with the initial phase and had started trading coffee at the ECX platform, we realized that the average quality of coffee that arrived last year and those arriving in the current year showed remarkable progress. The quality in the initial year used to be more in the 6–8 levels, whereas after the first year it used to be in the 4–7 range. Coffee being a perennial crop, the only way the quality can improve so quickly is through better post-harvest handling. The lesson learned was that if we incentivize the farmer for quality, he will take care of it.

These are intertwined issues, as there was no objective method or way to determine quality in regular practice. It was very easy for a buyer to refuse or make a default on the trade by citing poor quality. The farmer had no option but to accept the quality decided by the buyer as the final one, however subjective it may be. I was talking once to a trade expert in India who said a very interesting thing. He said that six months of effort, sweat, and blood from the farmer are tossed up in the air to conclude that the product is not good enough for a buyer. It is the most convenient thing to cite poor quality and enforce huge discounts on the farmer, who, in the system, is the weakest stakeholder. Unfortunately, farmers, in many countries, still remain price takers because of the inefficiencies in the market. The people benefiting from these inefficiencies always want the market to remain as inefficient as it is and do not encourage any type of restructuring. The recent farm law protest in India is also an example of the same. No effort that will balance the market power structure is ever welcome in an inefficient market.

Overall, in Ethiopia, the grain handling cost also used to be extremely high, and this extremely high handling cost meant that the farmers would get a smaller percentage of the overall grain trade value. In some cases, farmers used to get less than 25% of the value that the ultimate consumer was paying. The remaining 75% went into the handling cost. No wonder, in many countries in sub-Saharan Africa, the post-harvest losses stands at a staggering 20 to 25%, which means that just by addressing the handling cost and handling storage infrastructure properly, the productivity of the country can be increased by at least 20%. In the past, most of the countries in Africa promoted the concept of marketing boards, where it was planned that governments should create huge infrastructure and distribute food to consumers through these storage places. However, by the 1990s, the global donors and the World Bank started to champion the market-based economy model and started dismantling commodity and agriculture boards and corporations.

This started to happen throughout Africa. Eventually, it meant that, though there is huge infrastructure for storage available in the country, there was no business model that actually allows this infrastructure to be used for the benefit of post-harvest handling. It's an irony that, in spite of having a sufficient quantity of physical infrastructure, African agriculture even today faces significant challenges in post-harvest handling. I have worked in many countries after Ethiopia, and country after country, I have realized that the challenges remain the same. Infrastructure exists but exists within government parastatals, which are unable to put forward a market solution or a business model for this infrastructure to be used in a sustainable manner. These places remain idle, whereas the agricultural produce is exposed to losses due to the unavailability of the infrastructure.

Ethiopia had a similar problem. All-in-all, Ethiopia was, back in 2002–2004, faced with the significant challenge of market order. As Dr. Eleni puts it, there were a lot of inefficiencies in the market that had to be addressed. Issues ranged from contract default to post-harvest handling infrastructure to trust in trade and the inability of the traders to go beyond their known circles to trade, making markets fragmented. All these factors contributed to the fragmented and subdued market for agricultural commodities in Ethiopia. Dr. Eleni, through her 2005 paper, put forward a solution to these perineal problems in the form of a commodity exchange in Ethiopia. By 2005, she had already established an IFPRI office in Addis Ababa and was working aggressively on making policymakers understand the importance of market-driven infrastructure and a liberalized trade model for the overall agricultural development of Ethiopia.

Ethiopia was, in that period, becoming an economic powerhouse. Thanks to the leadership of Prime Minister Meles Zenawi He was, in that period, one of the strongest African leaders and had a very clear idea about the challenges and possible solutions for the country. He was willing to explore uncharted paths that would offer a long-term solution to the long-standing challenges in Ethiopian agriculture. He was assisted by the then deputy prime minister, Addisu Leggasy, who was also the agriculture minister. The commodity exchange was put forward as a solution by Dr. Eleni and Ian Goggin in their paper to the government of Ethiopia.

A commodity exchange is a market-based institution that brings order into the market by enforcing rules, creating infrastructure, and bringing trust into the trade. In most parts of the world, commodity exchanges are either set up by groups of traders or by investors from the private sector, who could see an opportunity in creating market-wide infrastructure for trade. The oldest commodity exchange in the world is the Chicago Board of Trade (CBOT), which was established to bring trust to the trade. The Chicago Board of Trade puts forward an excellent example of what a commodity exchange can achieve if it is done properly. The commodity exchange brings order into the market and aims to reduce the risk that is inherent to the agricultural trade. The origin of the Chicago Board of Trade is attributed to the fact that traders, who were worried about uncertain prices in the market, would in advance go to the market in Chicago and try to negotiate a deal that would give them the desired profit. The Chicago Board of Trade ensured that when such a price agreement is made, it is properly executed and people stand by their commitments in the trade. The Chicago Board of Trade was established as a futures trading platform. However, the same concept remains relevant to a spot market as well.

If the market institution can reduce the risk of default and offer remunerative opportunities to the traders, the markets will sustain. A commodity exchange is a rule-based system where pre-defined rules govern the markets.

All the participants are obliged to follow the rules, and those not following them are barred from participating. This rule-based system brings integrity and trust, as people are certain about the trade. A Commodity exchange is such an institution that, once established in the market, promotes this integrity. The process of a commodity exchange ensures that the quality of the product is ascertained in an objective manner and is fair to both buyers and sellers. This brings the much-needed quality certification process into the trade, which is normally missing. The model proposed by Dr. Eleni went a step forward and tried to create multiple market institutions under a single roof, which was needed in Ethiopia.

Traditionally, exchanges do not get involved in the physical handling of commodities, which in common language is called delivery systems. There are dedicated service providers who are approved by the exchanges to provide this service. However, in Ethiopia, such service providers were absent, and it required an integrated approach to develop such service providers along with the exchange. Hence, the model proposed by Dr. Eleni included warehousing and quality certification as integral components of the commodity exchange. There was a debate about the suitability of this model, and the global experts were, at that time as well as now, divided on the opinion of having warehousing and quality certification integrated into the exchange functions. Many thinkers believe that exchanges should run the exchange trading platform and leave market participants to develop other infrastructure. Whereas, other groups of experts believe that, for a country like Ethiopia, it is paramount that all the market-based institutions are developed together in an integrated manner. Both models have their own benefits and limitations, in my opinion. After working for 15 years in Africa, I have concluded that there is no one-size-fits-all solution. In Ethiopia, in 2005, the market challenges made it mandatory that the commodity exchange integrate warehousing and quality certification as integral parts. But in 2015, when I worked in Kenya, I concluded that there are existing institutions capable enough of handling this aspect, and as a result, a Kenyan commodity exchange may not need to replicate the Ethiopian model.

The paper by Dr. Eleni very effectively spelled out the benefits of a commodity exchange. This proposal of setting up the commodity exchange as a policy response to the food insecurity issues in Ethiopia was accepted by the government in 2006, and the official formal green light for the establishment of the commodity exchange in Ethiopia was given by the government. A task force was established under the chairmanship of Dr. Eleni, which did a detailed study to recommend policies and structures for the commodity exchange. The task force, in order to learn from the international experience, conducted a study tour to the Multi Commodity Exchange (MCX) in India, where I was working in May 2006. This was the first time that the Ethiopian effort collaborated with the Multi Commodity Exchange of India, which was to be carried forward in an extended relationship over the next few years. This delegation came to India, specifically to MCX, due to the relationship that Dr. Eleni had with Lemon Rutten, the then joint managing director at MCX. Dr. Eleni was depending a lot on international experience, and one of the experts she regularly consulted with was Lamon. The interest of MCX, which was a Financial Technologies-owned exchange, was to sell or partner with Ethiopia to set up the commodity exchange. Lamon, in all this, was an important figure in bringing the Ethiopian delegation to India. MCX and FT had by then gone out and set up such exchanges in Dubai and were looking to expand to Singapore and Johannesburg.

However, Dr. Eleni was smart enough to understand the implications of such a partnership and wanted to keep the exchange under government control. This was also driven by the fact that Ethiopia was a very controlled economy, and the exchange was to be part of a policy tool. By then, in Ethiopia, the private sector had still not been given the prominence it needed to run a market institution like the proposed commodity exchange. The government of Ethiopia approached various donors to support the commodity exchange project, and five donors—USAID, UNDP, the World Bank, IFAD, and Canadian Aid—agreed to pool close to three million dollars to kick-start the establishment of the commodity exchange in Ethiopia. It was out of this pool of funds that the capacity-building Workshops were sponsored in India and Ethiopia, where I participated as a trainer.

This was the background of the project before I was exposed to it during the training programs in 2007. Throughout 2007, stakeholder consultations, capacity building, and most importantly, identification of the key team were done by Dr. Eleni, operating through the IFPRI project in Addis Ababa. In my opinion, the biggest success that later enabled her to pull off such an ambitious project was her ability to pick the right team with the right skill sets. The initial team that was set up by Dr. Eleni was handpicked by her through her interactions in various countries. For a long period of time, Bemnet Aschenaki (Ben) was one of the very few expat members of the team before the other team members gradually joined in 2007 and early 2008. By the time I joined, the team was at full strength, and all required skill sets were within the team. We were all set to rock!

CHAPTER FIVE

The Road to Launch

After all my planning and formalities in India, I finally arrived in Ethiopia on February 10, 2008. As it was a Sunday, the work started on February 11, 2008. In fact, I was a bit late in joining the team, as most of the team members had already joined and work had already begun in full swing. I remember Dr. Eleni wanting me to join in early January, which I could not do due to the MCX. The office ECX operated from February 1st, 2008, was located in a government building called Buna Na Shay. It was a huge office occupied by the Coffee and Tea Authority. One floor in this building was allocated to the Ethiopia Commodity Exchange Project (ECX Project). This was a temporary office to operate from, as the AL-SAM building office was under constitution. The construction of the trading floor and the officers was in full swing at the AL-SAM building and was expected to take two months to complete. For this period of time, we had moved to the Buna Na Shay building to operate.

Prior to my arrival, a lot of work had been done in the preceding twelve to fifteen months, a lot of which I was aware of. The project, after its approval from the government in 2006, started working on putting together all the pieces of the commodity exchange, and capacity building was a part of that project plan. My interaction with the project started when the first batch of trainees arrived in India in February 2008. One of the most critical components of the exchange establishment is the structuring of the legal framework for the commodity exchange to operate. This was already done by the time I joined. Ethiopia was a country that did not have a stock exchange or any other type of financial exchange. The financial sector, specifically the capital market, was very rudimentary. It was a very controlled economy in terms of the financial industry, and the ministry of finance directly controlled the capital market operations. Without a stock exchange, the capital market in Ethiopia was the only primary market.

So, to introduce a commodity exchange, there were a lot of challenges. The concept of the exchange that was proposed required legal recognition through a legal enactment. Both the commodity exchange and the regulatory system were to be established. Though the project was looking after the commodity exchange establishment with little interference in the establishment of the regulatory authority, it was the government that was working on the regulatory body establishment. Two laws were enacted in Ethiopia, one pertaining to the establishment of the commodity exchange and the other to the establishment of the commodity exchange regulator. Though, in my opinion, a single act authorizing the establishment of the commodity exchange and the regulator could have been introduced, considering the Ethiopian legal system, having two separate proclamations was considered the best way forward.

The lawyers for the project decided to go that way. With the enactment in place between late 2007 and early 2008, the required legal infrastructure for the establishment of the exchange and its regulator was in place. Now all focus was on the exchange to be established. The work towards the exchange's establishment was in full swing. The exchange membership drive was the first formal interaction of the exchange with the prospective members. It was decided that hundred initial members would be recruited, who would be paying the birr equivalent of $5000 for the membership. This was especially an important task, as the private sector was totally unaware of what an exchange is and how an exchange would work. There was a lot of mystery surrounding the exchange. Though some leaders of the private sector had undergone significant training in India and many others in Ethiopia, for the public at large a lot of things were unknown.

The membership drive was launched on January 15th, 2008, in an event held at the Hilton Hotel in Addis Ababa at 6 p.m. At this time, since I was considered a member of the team, I was also invited to attend. The membership response was good, and by March 2008, ECX had 67 members registered out of the initial target of hundred. In an economy where no formal concept of exchange existed and the first ever exchange was established in less than three years, achieving 67% of your targeted membership number was no small achievement by any means. I remember that after I reached it, I learned how Dr. Eleni and Ben toiled day and night to get the required number of members registered. Of course, behind this success there was a push from the government as well, who wanted this exchange to be successful and be a benchmark in the East Africa region. The success of the recruitment drive gave a big boost to the overall exchange establishment drive.

In February 2008, after I arrived, the first assignment I was given was to be part of the recruitment interview team that was going to conduct marathon recruitment interviews for three to four days. An HR Consulting firm was hired by ECX to facilitate the large-scale recruitment of team members who would play critical roles in each department. The interviews were scheduled from February 12th to the whole week, and I was on multiple critical area panels. I was asked to conduct interviews for candidates in critical areas like trading, risk management, compliance, and membership. It was a great experience to interview candidates and select the appropriate one for each department.

I was to look after trading and was lucky to have a wonderful manager to work as my deputy. He called Abenet Bekele. Abenet was a perfect match for the trading floor, as he came from the hospitality industry but was very smart and particular about rules. So he had the perfect match that a trading floor manager requires, where he must be strict at the same time, should have a customer service approach, as he would be facing traders on the trading floor. Abenet was just that. Over the years, with ECX, Abenet grew to the level of Chief strategy officer and was one of the longest-serving members of the senior management team.

The launch date was fixed to be late March or early April, which was just about one and a half months from my arrival in Ethiopia. It was an elaborate launch process that would have a national forum and mock trading sections before the actual trading began. However, launch readiness was to be completed before the end of March. In my opinion, it was a very ambitious target. One of the critical components of the exchange was the technology. As I had discussed earlier, the initial design of the technology was developed internally. The team working on this had a good understanding of the ERP models and was working on the technology design for the exchange. The initial plan was to prepare a technology through assistance offered by the World Bank as a part of the fund allocated for ECX. However, Dr. Eleni realized quickly that buying a technology may not be a suitable option, as it will require a lot of capital outlay and will not be able to respond to market needs as soon as it goes live. Whenever any new market is established, the processes are designed based on a theoretical expectation of the market.

However, when the market starts operating and realistic challenges start emerging, one has to be very adaptive and responsive to the market and make necessary changes in the operating and functional aspects of the process to enable better accommodation of the market realities. I always believe that the best technology is the one that suits you and allows you to take the market development agenda forward, rather than asking the market to adjust to the technology platform that you have installed. This idea was the inspiration behind the decision of the ECX to build its own technology platform and give up the idea of procuring the technology from vendors like financial technologies in India.

In my earlier discussion, I had pointed out that one of the major interests that MCX had in the establishment of the commodity exchange in Ethiopia, besides training, was being a partner in ownership by providing technology. The model MCX was offering, based on my understanding, was that MCX would partner with ECX on a technology platform, and the monetary value of the technology platform would be considered an equity contribution by MCX. MCX would thus be an equity shareholder in the ECX. However, Ethiopia being the country that it is, a private sector player holding equity stakes in a commodity exchange was simply not acceptable, that too a foreign company. This meant that the only option left was to procure technology from MCX or the FT.

However, Eleni understood that the procurement of technology may severely limit her financial and operational capacities as the market would not be responsive as it should be. So, the decision was made to build its own technology platform. This task was given to Javad Ali, who worked on the initial design of the technology, along with one more team member, who eventually became the CIO of the exchange, Solomon Eddosa. In addition to this, there was a team of several highly talented Ethiopian technology and IT experts who were working on developing the platform for the ECX. Since the decision was made that the exchange would operate on a trading floor model, the complexity of the technology was not very high. It was merely an ERP system that could record and process the data of the trades taking place on the exchange floor.

This trading floor operation was my responsibility, and I, with the help of Ben, played a major role in developing the operational design of the floor. A detailed process on how the representatives of the traders would enter the floor, how they would use the hand signals, and how the tickets would be executed and submitted was developed. These were the few things for which I had to lay out a detailed step-by-step process for the physical trading floor. The floor was built on the second floor of the AL-SAM building. This floor was designed for public access, as it had the trading floor, the room for representatives of the traders, and the back office for trading, clearing and settlement, and central depository functions. The membership function was also given space on the second floor.

When you talk about the trading floor, the first image that flashes through your mind is that of the Chicago Board of Trade. The Chicago Board of Trade, by far, is the benchmark exchange for commodities in the world and has the iconic octagonal trading floor, where trades are negotiated between the brokers or their representatives through physical interaction. Since ECX was going to follow the same model, it was decided that the floor of the exchange would also be built in an octagonal design. Dr. Eleni, for that matter, was very particular about aesthetics and had an amazing sense of the impact that aesthetics carried. She knew that this floor would be visited by a lot of people from within and outside the country, and an octagonal trading floor would immediately link it to the Chicago Board of Trade. This will definitely add credibility to the work that Ethiopia is doing. I had seen this actually play out when dignitaries visited the ECX.

Now that the technology and staff issues have been addressed, it is important to focus attention on the detailed processes. The development of the process was happening individually between the departments and was stitched together into a seamlessly flowing end-to-end process. This work was assigned to another member of the team, Mike Kinfu. Mike used to spend a lot of time with the different departments, understanding their processes, and then integrating them into one seamless flow. It was a big help that he himself was also working on the warehouse and quality management processes, which were the most complex.

One of the major challenges that ECX had to overcome was the challenge of executing the financial settlement for trades. In those days, the National Bank of Ethiopia did not have a central clearing system. It used to take more than two weeks to clear inter-bank transfers, and in such an environment, building a system that would enable settlements to take place on the next day of trade seemed almost impossible. However, this was achieved by designing a system that paved the way for the launch of a national payment system a few years later by the National Bank of Ethiopia. This task was given to a team member called Keith Thomas. Keith was a financial sector expert, and based on the London metal exchange model, he developed a clearing and settlement solution that would enable the exchange to settle the trades almost immediately, on the next day, with banks able to exchange the funds in an inter-bank structure.

I remember that, when I had joined, within a week's time, the management team was invited by the Deputy Prime Minister to meet and introduce themselves. This meeting was requested by Dr. Eleni, and we all got a chance to meet and introduce ourselves to the Deputy Prime Minister of Ethiopia, Ato Addisu Legasse. In that meeting, the Deputy Prime Minister was very appreciative of the decision we had taken to come to Ethiopia and help Ethiopia build the commodity exchange. He also warned us that working in Ethiopia would be different from working in any western part of the world, where a lot of things can be taken for granted. I remember him taking out a pen from his pocket and telling me, "Gentleman, to get this pen in your pocket may also be an elaborate process in Ethiopia, so please bear with us and do not be demotivated if you find things not happening at the pace at which they would in your part of the world." Over the years in ECX, I realized what he meant!

We were moving in full swing towards the launch date, which was still open and expected to be at the end of March or early April. With momentum building up due to the recruitment of members, the launch date was eagerly anticipated by both the government and the market. Though it was a government project supported by donors, it had no peculiarities of a government project or a donor-driven project. In fact, it was more like a start-up company with very tight deadlines to meet. By mid-February, we were in full swing toward the launch. Dr. Eleni had taken over as interim CEO as the company formally got registered in late February or early March. The Board of directors was almost formed. By then, the construction of the building, specifically the trading floor and other critical facilities for the launch, had reached its finish line, and by the middle of March, it was expected to be done.

Members had already been recruited and were being trained for the trading protocols. The staff that was critical for the operational launch was also in place, and their training was also going on. It was agreed that by the end of March, the mock trading should happen. This was all a very exciting time in ECX, and I had no time to think about being lonely in Ethiopia or having time to develop any social contacts to keep me busy. The work itself was keeping me busy, as we would invariably have late evening meetings running into the night and the full day spent working on our deliverables towards the launch.

One of the important outreach activity that was to be done was organizing a national forum. This national forum would be the official announcement of ECX by the government, and it was expected that the national forum would be addressed by the prime minister himself. Initially, the dates were set for March 24–26, and it was expected to have close to 2,000 people attend the national forum. This was going to be a huge event that would announce the formal launch of the ECX. This forum was to present to the stakeholders the ECX's readiness, its business model, and its technology, and possibly give them an experience of how they would trade. I was, honestly, shell-shocked when I heard that I would be speaking in front of 2,000 people and presenting the business model for the trading operations. As if this was not enough, Dr. Eleni very casually said, "***Bharat, let's have the big trading simulation that you do in trainings for the entire group.***"

The trading simulation I had earlier done during the training program was for a maximum of thirty five to forty people. In my life, I had never handled a larger group than fifty participants. Now, doing a trading simulation for two thousand people was, for me, beyond possibility. Still, I did not respond to Dr. Eleni at that point in time, but I knew that if she mentioned it, it was going to happen. Finally, the national forum was organized on April 4th and 5th, 2008. The national forum was a huge initiative and was attended by close to fifteen hundred participants. These people represented farmers, their cooperatives, exporters, traders, agribusinesses, financial institutions like banks and insurance companies, government agencies, government ministries, donor agencies, and diplomats. Almost everybody was in the room.

It was one of the most proud moments for me till then, as I had never been a part of such a mega event in my life as a speaker. More importantly, I was going to speak on that platform where the Deputy Prime Minister would be present. Speaking in front of fifteen hundred people from such a platform was enough to give me a lot of anxiety and nerves. I had prepared my presentation, and, though I was confident in this subject, just the fact that I had to speak to fifteen hundred people was unbelievable. The forum was inaugurated by His Excellency Meles Zanavi, the Prime Minister of Ethiopia, and was championed by the Deputy Prime Minister, who was the government mentor of an ECX in the system. The national forum was called "***Creating a Market for All***", pretty much on the lines of what we were trying to do.

During the functional sessions, we were sitting on the podium, which was approximately seven to ten feet above the ground, with fifteen hundred people sitting in front of us. This was held at the Economic Commission for Africa (UN-ECA), which was one of the very few places to have such a huge infrastructure in Addis Ababa. When my chance came to present the trading floor operations through the PowerPoint presentation that I had prepared, surprisingly, I was able to go through the presentation very comfortably and coolly. I was able to explain how the trading floor would operate. However, the bigger challenge was yet to come. I have mentioned that Dr. Eleni, in one of the management meetings, talked about conducting a mock trading session, or a trading simulation, as she called it, for the participants of the forum. For about thousand people, conducting a trading simulation seemed virtually impossible for me. However, saying that was not an option, and I had to figure out how to design the trading simulation. I kept thinking about it and was able to figure it out at lunch on day one.

The lunch was served in a big hall that had seating capacity for about thousand people who could sit around on round tables. There were three rows of tables, with twenty tables each, each table having fifteen seats around it to sit. I quickly did my math and decided that I would get the middle row removed and add five seats to each table, making it twenty seats. This would mean we have an area with forty tables, with space in the middle. Each table would represent one team, and we would have four rounds of simulation trading, which meant that one representative from each team would come on the floor. The middle open space was designated as the trading floor. This way, we would have forty people, and managing forty people on the floor was doable, as I had done it before.

Finally, by the evening of day one, I was peaceful as I had figured out a way to address this challenge. Little did I know that the challenge was still there. On day two, after lunch, I asked the ECX team at the venue to get the arrangements done as per the design I had planned. I explained to them that they should get the middle rows removed and increase the seats in the two corner rows. I went back to the forum, seemingly confident that things would be done. However, something in me told me to go and check it so that I do not have surprises when we go for the simulation. As I reached the hall, I realized that the team was removing the two rows on the outside, leaving the central row intact! Exactly the opposite of what I had told. My heart was in my mouth, as at any time people might come into the room for simulation, and we were in a very awkward arrangement. Immediately, I asked the team to redo the arrangement and personally supervised the arrangements to be done in the way they were planned.

Eventually, before the people could come in, the room's arrangements were done, and we were ready for this simulation. As I was about to start, I asked for the microphone. I was told that the room does not have a public announcement system. So, I have to work and talk to thousand people without the microphone. I quickly relied on the strengths of my vocal cords and started shouting at the top of my voice. I realized that day how strong a voice I have! No more surprises, and the rest of the simulation went very smoothly, and the experience that people had was something that they carried with them for a long time. I also had a sore throat for a few days, but the satisfaction was more comforting than the pain.

For some people, it was the first time in their lives that they had played a trading game like this, and they were very excited about the whole process. They very quickly learned how to use their hands for signalling and how to negotiate the trade on the floor. This, I believe, was an important icebreaker that gave them confidence about the exchange and its process and made them comfortable about participating in the exchange. None of my colleagues ever thought that this would go so smoothly, as everybody was having the same thought as I had in the initial days: how will we have thousands of people participating in the trading game? Finally, I was able to achieve it. Everyone, especially Dr. Eleni, was full of praise for me. One of the colleagues congratulated me, saying "you have a golden touch". I was overwhelmed with the achievement I had that day.

With the national forum now done and formerly ECX being announced, we were getting into the business end of the project. Daily, we were having meetings to ensure we were on track and everything was under control. For the launch, a detailed action plan was drawn, which included the opening of the warehouse before the trade was to begin. It was in mid-April that the warehouse operations were launched and the first deposit was received at ECX warehouses. A total of more than 300 bags of maize were deposited in the ECX Warehouse in Addis Ababa a week before trading could begin. By now, we had set the 24th of April as our date for the first trade on ECX to take place. The 24th of April was a big day in my life and will always remain that way, as that day was mainly my show as the action shifted from the warehouse to the trading floor. We had worked very hard to reach where we were and were pretty confident that things would happen as they were planned. From the 10th of February 2008, when I arrived in Ethiopia, to this date, memories flashed in my mind about everything that I did to reach this day.

When I arrived, the trading department was supervised by Ben, in addition to the business development and membership that he was looking into. Initially, I and Ben worked together on developing the trading floor operations before he got too consumed with the business development work. By then, I had also settled down, started to pick up responsibility independently, and developed all the systems that were necessary for the trading floor. We had a trading floor manager and the data entry clerks in place, who would be critical for this operation. Finally, on the morning of

April 24, the bell rang at the exchange for the first time, and the buyers and sellers started negotiating. They were not reaching an agreement, and the session time was running out. I was praying to God to make that first trade happen. Just before the closing bell, I heard a clap and buyer and seller shaking hands for the trade! Finally, a sale was recorded between Luma Adama Cooperative and Syed Yaseen PLC.

This was a historic day for Ethiopia, the exchange, and for me personally, as I had achieved something that I never thought I would achieve. With the trading session finally done and the exchange operations formally launched, it was time for me to go back home to Mumbai, India, and work on relocating my family to Ethiopia.

CHAPTER SIX

TEAM MEMBERS

As it is said that Rome was not built in a day, the ECX was also not built in a day. It was the toiling effort of several people for several months before the exchange could start trading on April 24, 2008. Of course, the concept and the groundwork were done by Dr. Eleni, but it was not Dr. Eleni alone who built the commodity exchange. A team of close to twenty people worked with Dr. Eleni to make the exchange trade's first warehouse receipt.

Dr. Eleni had some very strong traits in her personality, which made it possible to convince the policymakers by selling a very compelling story about the commodity exchange. Also, she was able to get the donors excited about the project and ready to contribute to the establishment. I remember one incident that gives an idea of the thought process and confidence in the project. A donor agency that was not on the initial donor list wanted to join as a donor after the ECX had established its mark. The representative of the donor agency, an European, came to the exchange, seeking to meet Dr. Eleni. Dr. Eleni was busy and could not meet him. He was politely told to come some other day. He was not amused and insisted on meeting her the same day. He was very upset and talked about having the funds for ECX. Dr. Eleni told him that there are many more donors lining up for ECX, and ECX does not want his support. He was taken aback, as he was not expecting that. Later, he made peace with Dr. Eleni and agreed to ECX terms. Dr. Eleni has this uncanny knack of getting what she wants.

She had a lot of passion for building the commodity exchange, and this passion was very critical for achieving the speed with which the ECX was established. Another unique quality that Dr Eleni had was that she was able to assemble a team with the right skill sets for the work to be achieved. Most of the team members were personally known to Dr. Eleni. Initially, the project had international and local Ethiopian consultants who were working on the commodity exchange concept and its groundwork with stakeholders and the government. The project needed more local staff. But as ECX was established, eventually the top management of ECX was made up of diaspora and technical experts who brought a global outlook to the exchange being established.

The oldest member of the team was Bemnet Aschenaki, or Ben, as we would always call him. Ben was known to Dr. Eleni when the project was in its very initial stages. Ben had an successful background working with brokerage houses like Merrill Lynch in the United States. He used to work on the trade floor of the broking house and had a very strong understanding of trading and exchange operations. Ben was also well-versed in the Ethiopian agricultural trade background, as he came from a family that used to be agricultural traders and exporters for a long time. So not only the understanding but also the network that Ben had in the trading community in Ethiopia was a big asset for ECX to have. I first met Ben when he came to India with the training participants in February 2007.

I instantly connected with Ben, as I found him very diligent, honest, and polite. It was easy to communicate with him, and he would be very appreciative of what we were doing. He would also guide us to ensure that the participants expectations and our delivery match. He was in charge of training in the project phase, and all three training programs that I conducted through MCX were overseen by Ben. When I landed in Ethiopia, Ben was the person I was working with, and he had helped me settle down quickly into the ECX system. Even today, I continue to be in touch with Ben and have a lot of respect for his professionalism and the experience he carries.

Along with Ben, the second-oldest member of the team was Messarat Nega. She was a qualified lawyer who worked with the Securities Exchange Commission in the United States of America. Her exposure to the Securities Exchange Commission was a big asset for ECX to have, as she played a vital role in developing the proclamations and negotiating them with the government for their enactments. She also worked on the rulebook of the exchange, which, in my opinion, was very effectively drafted. Given the fact that there were no reference points in Ethiopia, as no exchange ever existed in Ethiopia, Drafting the rulebook was very challenging. At that time, not many benchmarks in Africa existed for ECX to refer to. However, she did not continue beyond the launch, and as the exchange entered into the next phase in July 2008, Messarat had moved out of ECX.

Messarat was replaced by another equally qualified lawyer from the United States, Yohannes Assefa. Yohannes, like Messarat, was also a securities lawyer who had an illustrious career in the legal field in the United States. He was a member of the diaspora community, and in the offer, he saw an opportunity to make a difference in the country of his birth. Dr. Eleni had met him during her US visit in July 2008, and Yohannes decided to relocate to Ethiopia to serve his country of birth. Yohannes, in my opinion, was very sharp and pragmatic. When it came to the key legal and regulatory approaches, as the head of compliance, he did a wonderful job ensuring that the rule of law was enforced in the exchange. Yohannes and I worked a lot together, and I found him someone who would bring a lot of energy and thought into the system. Yohannes played a critical role when coffee was introduced into the system and there were issues where the rule of law was to be enforced. Not only with the participants but also with the government, Yohannes did it wonderfully. Even after our ECX days, I and Yohannes continue to work together and still have a very strong bond between us.

The next area that required a lot of technical expertise was building the clearing and settlement system. The clearing and settlement system was to be built in an environment where there was no reference point since there was no stock exchange in Ethiopia. By then, the clearing and settlement systems were totally unknown to the banks. In an environment where banks would take three to four days to clear intra-bank checks, asking them to do a fund transfer in less than forty eight hours with multiple banks in play was something the banks laughed about and said this could not be done. But eventually, on day one of exchange trading on April 24, it was done. By then, Ethiopia, or the National Bank of Ethiopia, did not have the national payment clearing systems, or the clearing house, as central banks call it, which meant that interbank clearing was a big hassle. It was because of the success of ECX clearing and settlement systems that the National Bank of Ethiopia decided to launch the project to build a national clearing system.

Dr. Eleni knew that if someone had to develop such a system, he must be highly qualified and technically sound. Dr. Eleni found such an expert in the form of Keith Thomas. Keith was working on some projects in Ethiopia, and Dr. Eleni offered him to work on this project, which Keith found very exciting. Keith had a very strong technology and banking background, because of which he was able to understand the complexity of the solution that was required to be put forward. His technical expertise and understanding of the banking systems made it easy for ECX to convince the banks to be part of the system. The system Keith developed remained the backbone of the exchange as it went into the next stage of development. My first interaction with Keith happened in November 2007, when I was in Ethiopia for this second training program that we were conducting. Keith discussed with me the way it is done in India, and I was more than happy to share with him more details, even after my return from Ethiopia. I shared with him the MCX circular, which explains the clearing and settlement system, and a few other relevant write-ups that I could find in India. In ECX, my office was outside Keith's office, and anybody going to his office had to pass through my office. I usually used to joke with Keith that I was his gatekeeper.

It was not only complicated processes that were to be developed for operations, but converting those complicated processes into technology-enabled solutions was a bigger task. ECX decided that it would not go for an expensive technology suit but rather build its own technology platform using its requirements as specifications. The initial task was assigned to Javad Ali. Jawad was a technocrat from the United States with a very good understanding of ERP systems. He did the system analysis and design for the ECX technology suit and presented it to the team in mid-February 2008. He explained the technology in very simple language, and I was particularly impressed with the way he had developed it. However, after doing this, Jawad left, and the baton was handed over to another equally qualified technical expert, Solomon Eddosa. I had met Solomon, like Keith, in November 2007. At that time, Solomon had just started working on the project and was trying to understand the platform that MCX was using.

Solomon's task in the initial days was very tough, as the processes were not getting streamlined and kept changing. This meant that Solomon's work remained exposed to a lot of changes. Solomon was leading a team of experts from Ethiopia, and it was not only the technology development but also the networking, hardware, and anything related to IT that was Solomon's responsibility. Solomon had come to Ethiopia after a noted career in the IT sector in the United States. He worked for Accenture and was part of several projects of very high importance. Solomon would spend a lot of time understanding the process so that he could make it easy for his team to develop a solution around that process. This kept me and Solomon in very close contact, as I was invariably involved in developing processes for the exchange. I and Solomon also worked on a technology procurement bid, which was floated in 2009 and 2010. Both bids, unfortunately, were not successful. We had spent considerable time evaluating these bids together.

In the initial days, it was important for the project to have someone who would stitch the different processes together and make them flow seamlessly. This responsibility was given to Mike Kinfu, who was a senior business consultant from the United States. Mike had worked for multiple years in business process development and strategic planning with organizations like Accenture. Mike was a very soft-spoken but very sharp guy to work with. He was also given the additional responsibility of leading the warehouse operations, which were critical to the exchange. Though some of the processes for warehouse operations and quality certifications were developed by external consultants, Mike's role was to ensure that these operations flowed smoothly. Mike did not continue with the exchange beyond the initial phase and opted out immediately after the exchange was launched.

In the second phase, when the exchange was going for coffee and sesame trading and in super expansion mode, Mike's role was assigned to another individual from the United States who had a recognized career in revenue management and logistics: Aman Addinu. He was, like most of the members of the team, an Ethio-American, an entrepreneur at heart, and a senior business practitioner. Aman joined us somewhere in September and was assigned the responsibility of being the in charge of the warehousing operations, where the warehouse operations and the quality-related aspects were under his supervision. Aman worked tirelessly to develop the delivery model for coffee and later sesame, which required a lot of hard work and innovation. Eventually, after his ECX days, Aman is today a successful coffee farmer, trader, and exporter.

An important aspect of the commodity exchange was market data information systems, which meant that the information generated by the exchange would be publicly made available. This was an independent division in itself, and Dr. Eleni had identified a technical expert to run this department. At the same time, when I joined in February, another expert, whose name was Ahadu Woubshet, joined. He was an Ethio-American with a very strong IT and market data background. Before joining ECX, he was running the market data displays on the Fannie Mae's trading floor. He had particular experience relevant to the commodity exchange and proved to be a valuable asset to the company. I found her to be a very happy-go-lucky type of character who would be very serious with his work but equally enjoy life outside of work. Sometimes, his social lifestyle in Ethiopia made some eyebrows rise, but I found him to be a wonderful person to be with. When it came to work, he had exceptional skills to deliver what was expected of him professionally. I thought he was a go-getter and would achieve whatever he was tasked with doing. This approach proved very helpful when, in the interim, he was given the charge to run the warehouse operations along with market data.

The last role was that of a risk expert. An individual called Michele Brhane was given the responsibility of developing and maintaining the risk register for ECX and was in charge of risk and surveillance at the exchange. Though it was a floor exchange, surveillance was not very technical. Still, there was a staff member who reported to Michele Brahne for surveillance. Mike was also from the Ethiopian diaspora in the United States and had experience with KPMG. He was not somebody who would speak a lot but was very humble and down-to-earth. However, one of his casual statements after the launch made him run into trouble with Dr. Eleni. This eventually played a role in Michele Brhane and Mike Kinfu not opting for the next round of appointments and a continuing role with ECX.

The exchange was more in a start-up mode, and people were given responsibilities that did not always pertain to their role at work. Michele, along with risk management, was given the responsibility of finance and corporate service. In one of the meetings, Michele voiced his discontent by saying "This is not what I signed up for". These words were not taken kindly by Dr. Eleni, and she shot back through an email, which caused a lot of stir in the management team. I was in India at the time, and, honestly, as an Indian, I did not see that this email had any problems. In India, we are unfortunately used to bosses using harsh words in their communications and emails. However, this was not the case, especially with the senior experts from the United States, as it was considered unprofessional by them. Over the years, when I think of this incident, I realize that it was more of a clash of personalities than anything else.

Dr. Eleni had a very strong personality and would not like any sort of challenge in her management team. However, some members of the management team, including Michele Brahne and Mike Kinfu, thought otherwise and would not take such harsh communication lying down. The discontent in the management team eventually subsided superficially, but led to the withdrawal of Michele Brahne and Mike Kinfu from the management team.

After a few weeks of my arrival in Ethiopia, I asked Dr. Eleni about the continuation. I was prepared to be back in India after the initial period of six months was over in July 2008. To my surprise, Dr. Eleni told me that there is a possibility that the next one will be offered employment by the government of Ethiopia. UNDP was supporting the ECX. One of the forms of support was technical assistance. The appointment was to be through this technical assistance project. In this case, UNDP would pay the government of Ethiopia the funds that the Government of Ethiopia would use to pay the salaries of technical experts like me. For me, it was welcome information. However, Dr. Eleni also said that the modalities are being worked out, and she would prefer the appointments to be made directly under the UNDP umbrella rather than through the government route.

The final modalities worked out between the Government of Ethiopia and the UNDP were that the UNDP would recruit technical experts and second them to the ECX. For UNDP to recruit anyone, it was important that the person be a foreigner. Six positions, including the CEO and five others, were advertised by UNDP in late May for recruitment. These positions included the CEO, the Head of trading operations, the head of risk management, the CIO, the head of market data, and the head of warehousing and quality certification. Dr. Eleni, myself, Solomon, and Ahadu applied for the respective positions that we were holding and hoped to cross over into the UNDP contract. The UNDP had made it amply clear that it would be a competitive recruitment process, and we had to go through this competitive process in order to secure our appointments. Though our previous experience gave us an edge, there was no guarantee that we would be the finally selected candidate.

However, we made it to the cut after being shortlisted and subsequently clearing the interviews. For the remaining two positions, head of risk management and head of warehousing, for which Michele Brahne and Mike Kinfu withdrew their applications, UNDP could not find an acceptable candidate for warehouse operations. whereas the risk role was assigned to a British Ghanaian citizen, Dr. Kadri Alfah. Dr. Kadri had previous experience working with the London Stock Exchange and was more than capable of replacing Michele Brahne. Eventually, Dr. Kadri was given the additional responsibility of running the central depository operations. He proved his worth in the organization and ensured that the exchange risk was properly managed. Later in his career, Dr. Kadri went on to become the Country representative and head of the commodity exchanges in Rwanda and later the founding CEO of the commodity exchange in Ghana.

Under USAID assistance, four positions were recruited. The head of business development, the head of compliance, the head of clearing and settlement, and the chief finance officer were recruited. The first three positions were held by the same people, Ben, Yohannes, and Keith, respectively; the CFO role was given to Yonas. He was also a wonderful addition to the team.

There was a strategy to plan for succession, as the government had made it amply clear that they would like to see Ethiopians running the exchange. As a result, the technical experts, recruited under the UNDP and USAID, were to be phased out in three years' time. We had a very strong team of managers working with each of us. These managers were groomed for three years under each functional head and were expected to take over when we, the expats, leave. However, this strategy was blown away in January 2011 when substantial changes in the exchange management structure were made by Dr. Eleni.

CHAPTER SEVEN

SMELLING THE COFFEE

After the launch of trading on April 24, 2008, the initial fanfare was over, and now we were getting down to business. The exchange required regular trades to ensure that the business picked up following the launch. However, it was not easy, and we were finding it difficult week after week to conduct the trading sessions. It was decided that after the initial launch, the exchange would not trade on a daily basis but have one trading day a week. So the weekly trading would mean that the volumes accumulated over the time that could be traded, and the exchange would have sufficient time to gather traction. Ben was struggling hard to ensure that deposits were in the warehouse and were offered for trade.

Though some deposits were coming into the warehouse, they were not in sufficient quantity for trading. It was becoming more and more difficult. There were times when the trading session was postponed to ensure that the participants reached the exchange and the exchange had a trading session. Even if two or three traders turned up to the session, we would not have trades agreed upon, and it took a long time for the exchange to register the next trade after the first trade on April 24th, 2008. This was not a particularly good time for us.

We knew that this was the beginning of a long road to success. Nowhere in the world has any exchange, right from day one, tasted success, and this was the only fact that kept us going. Though the government had put its weight behind us, and the deputy prime minister was the biggest advocate of the commodity exchange in the government, there were many in the government that would be super appreciative of the exchange concept, but in their hearts, they were waiting to see the signs of failure.

In any structured market in a developing economy, especially in the agriculture market sector, a lot of inefficiencies are found, and these inefficiencies inherently benefit the traders rather than the smallholder farmers. As a result, none of the traders wants this inefficiency to go away and the market to be more efficient and transparent. Ethiopia was not different. There were structural inefficiencies that the traders wanted to reserve, and the exchange was trying to address them. Getting support from traders was difficult, if not impossible.

Not only that, we were also facing challenges due to rising commodity prices. In Ethiopia, 2007 and 2008 were bad years for its food security. Ethiopia was facing the challenge that the exchange wanted to address, and now the same was becoming a challenge for the exchange. For global food prices, this was also a bad time, as global food prices had significantly increased in 2007 and in the first and second quarters of 2008. There was a global food crisis in the making. A lot of this crisis happened because of escalating food prices globally. This was because of multiple factors. There was a drought in 2006. Also, oil prices increased significantly, which led to an increase in the cost of fertilizer and industrial agriculture. This rising cost of fertilizers meant that countries like Ethiopia could not afford fertilizers, and as a result, productivity went down.

This was not a good time to start a commodity exchange. We were caught in the global headwinds immediately upon launch. This was a time when commodity prices were at an all-time high and there was a lot of inflationary pressure on agricultural commodities. During this time, the world average price of rice increased by more than 200% and that of wheat by more than 125%. The maize prices had also shot up by close to 225% globally. In April 2008, the rise in prices hit an all-time high in the United States, doubling the price in just seven months. The impact on Ethiopia was also very significant, and the grain prices in Ethiopia had also shown a 150–200% rise in prices by June 2008. The prices of wheat in Ethiopia had jumped up to ETB 600 per quintal, which used to be ETB 300 a year ago.

A lot of economists believe that this happened because of global population growth. However, in my opinion, it was the outcome of multiple factors that played a role. There was a lot of food insecurity across the globe, and this time, the world had also seen a lot of expansion into commercial agriculture, especially in Ethiopia. A lot of investors started investing in commercial agriculture, taking large parcels of land on lease from the government of Ethiopia for commercial cultivation. The land was offered at a very cheap lease rental, and investors made a beeline for the same.

All in all, it was just after our launch that we were caught in the global food crisis situation, making it a very difficult time for the exchange to sustain. There were a lot of thoughts going through the exchange management team on how to bring more volume and more trade to the Exchange. But, with inflationary trends very strong in Ethiopia, trade volumes themselves were dropping. This meant that the exchange opportunities were also shrinking, and we were struggling every passing day to get volumes on the exchange platform.

The inability of the exchange to generate sufficient volumes would mean that the exchange was very quickly becoming a white elephant, and the Board of Directors of the exchange, which was made up of private and public representatives, started to put pressure on Dr. Eleni to ensure that the exchange gained momentum. We were all brainstorming solutions for getting the exchange to profitability. A lot of thought went into what could bring the exchange into business, revive the confidence that the exchange had from policymakers and private stakeholders, and drive it towards profitability.

By June 2008, a lot of people who did not want the exchange to succeed started talking about the exchange being the reason for rising prices and that it was creating food insecurity in the country. The Board of the exchange was particularly worried about not only the profitability of the exchange but also the perception that was being created around it. They immediately wanted a quick reversal of this image, as if, in the initial days, an image was cast, then it would be very difficult for the exchange to change it into a positive perception of itself.

Having struggled with grains, understanding the diversity of the grain industry in Ethiopia, and more importantly, realizing the difficulty in breaking the inefficient structures, our thoughts started to revolve around other commodities. This led to a discussion on commodities like coffee and sesame. These were major export crops for the country. Being an export crop, there was a structured market design and a functioning value chain, which could be further improved by the introduction of the commodity exchange, we believed.

Dr. Eleni, very quickly realizing that grain may not be the best bet for the future, started focusing on export commodities like coffee and sesame. In the meantime, there was another option that was explored by the exchange. It was a time when Ethiopia was planning to import substantial quantities of wheat and distribute it at subsidized prices for food security. This initiative was to be led by the ministry of trade, and the minister, Girima Biru, was working very hard on it. He wanted to ensure that the deal was quickly approved and that the grains were imported as soon as possible to make them available in Ethiopia. Though it was a food security issue, the operations of the intervention were still trusted to the ministry of trade.

Dr. Eleni had very quickly identified this as an opportunity to bring exchange back into discussion, if exchange gets to play a role in this. I was tasked with the responsibility of designing a structure where the price stabilization mechanism adopted by the government, through the sale of imported wheat, can be facilitated through the commodity exchange. This market stabilization exercise was to be the largest market stabilization intervention in the history of Ethiopia. The intervention was planned to import 150,000 metric tons of wheat from the world market and sell it on the open market in Ethiopia at a fixed subsidized price in the next two months.

As you would know, open market operation is a distinct price stabilization instrument in which supplies are released in the market as a single injection of supply to all market actors indiscriminately, rather than a targeted rationing program. This open-market operation normally acts faster as it is easier to administer and is less prone to corruption. This was the strategy that Ethiopia was adopting under the leadership of the ministry of trade, led by Girima Biru.

I, along with Dr. Eleni and Paul Dorosh, an Economist from The World Bank, wrote a policy paper that justifies the role of the ECX in creating the distribution platform for sale to the local market through the exchange. When the market price had hit 600 Birr per Quintal, it was planned that the imported wheat would be sold at a fixed price of Birr 300 per quintal, and the announcement would be made two months prior. It is a well-known fact that not only the actual sale but the anticipation and the news of the sale coming, with the actual sale happening in the next few months, would also trigger some level of reaction in the market and help in bringing down or controlling the market prices.

We conducted a detailed simulation and explained by the statistical conclusion that the sale at a price of 350 Birr per quintal and the impact triggered in the market can push the price down to 265 Birr per quintal. We proposed a model that would include the exchange infrastructure. Since the commodity exchanges are designed to enable efficient and secure trading through an automated trading system and rapid order processing, including clearing and settlement, the ECX would be the right platform to sell the imported wheat into the market.

The Ethiopian Grain Trade Enterprise, or EGTE, was the authorized institution responsible for the importation, physical delivery, inventory management, and handling of the imported wheat for the intervention. We proposed that EGTE become a member of the exchange and sell the large quantity of wheat at a fixed price of 350 Birr per quintal into the market using the ECX platform. This would mean that the ECX would assist the EGTE in rapidly processing the transaction orders on a first-come, first-served basis and expediting the sale on the basis of standard lots and minimum order sizes. This would help to prevent market cornering by influential traders. ECX was capable of limiting the order size, which would mean that huge quantities of wheat could be sold within a single day.

Our estimates showed that ECX was capable of processing around 75,000 tons in a single day, which meant that the overall imported wheat of 150,000 tons could be sold off very quickly. In this model, it was also suggested that ECX can help make the market more stable by introducing futures trading. It was proposed that the EGTE can start selling in the market under a futures contract the huge quantities that it is scheduled to import and deliver in the next two months. A big price indication from the futures market would lead to market stabilization, and the commodity exchange would be able to help in bringing stability to the market much before these stocks have been arrived at and distributed.

This was a wonderful idea, in my opinion, and a very well-defined strategy. Myself, Dr. Eleni, and Paul were pretty confident that the Ethiopian government would like this model and, if not the futures market, at least use the ECX platform to trade in the spot market and use its large-scale order processing capacity for EGTE to quickly and efficiently make the sale. But, unfortunately, this paper never got government approval, and the ECX lost an opportunity to stamp its mark on the spot markets by showing its capacity in trading the imported wheat. Also, the opportunity to look into futures trading was almost lost.

This wheat was eventually imported and sold through conventional market mechanisms. The systems did not work, and eventually it was realized that the way the process was handled did not result in results. It failed to create the desired impact as the market had too many gaps. The time gap in the sale was huge, which resulted in the prices being absorbed by the traders. The sale was coming in small quantities and being offloaded in small quantities. This gave traders sufficient time to buy them and sell them back at higher prices before buying again from EGTE. Ultimately, this whole exercise did not have the desired impact. I still believe that had the Ethiopian government decided to trade through the ECX, a lot of success would have been achieved. I am not sure if this was because of the political differences between the leadership or any other reason, but eventually the ECX failed to capitalize on a huge opportunity that existed and would have changed the ECX's Fortunes in a very short span of time.

With the opportunity lost to trade in the imported wheat and the grain market, specifically wheat and maize, becoming too difficult to crack, We as a team started to look at other alternate crops where ECX can operate and create market opportunities. Two commodities, or products, that were proposed by Dr. Eleni were coffee and Sesame. Both were export-oriented crops, and Ethiopia exported huge quantities of these crops every year. However, cracking into the coffee and sesame markets was still more difficult because of the multiple challenges we faced in those commodities. The team's understanding of grains was very strong, and ECX was developed to trade grains rather than commercial crops like coffee and sesame. So, including coffee and sesame in trade would be a difficult route, and we believed that at such an initial stage of our existence, when even the grain market and the grain-related processes are not stabilized, getting into coffee or sesame would be a difficult decision. Most of the management team members were not very keen on the coffee and sesame idea.

Dr. Eleni believed that this was the only way forward. I guess she was facing pressure from the board and possibly pressure from the higher authorities in the government, who were very keen to see the exchange create some positive news rather than become a white elephant. The political weight that the prime minister and the deputy prime minister had put behind this project was now put to the test, and if this did not work out properly, there would be political repercussions. So, a decision was made after a lot of political discussions. Finally, it was agreed that coffee and sesame would be explored. After many other rounds of discussion, finally coffee was identified as the first commodity to be added to the ECX trading platform, and it was agreed that this season, which normally starts in November or December, would be the time when ECX started with coffee trading. This was the political decision. With the decision being made, there was a lot of work to be done from now until December, when the first coffee bean would be traded on the exchange platform. It seemed like we were again in start-up mode, with the coffee project staring at us.

Coffee is an integral part of Ethiopian culture. In Ethiopia, coffee is much more than a simple refreshing drink; it is a part of the cultural fabric of the country. It is a part of social rituals that unites friends, families, and neighbours in a shared experience. Coffee is called buna in Ethiopia. During my stay in Ethiopia, I had a chance to visit and participate in several coffee ceremonies.

Drinking coffee in Ethiopia is not like what we do in the USA or India; just go to the coffee vending machine, fill your cup, and drink it! It is an elaborate ritual that needs to be enjoyed and respected.

Celebrating the coffee ceremony in Ethiopia has various steps. There is roasting, then grinding the beans, then brewing the coffee in clay pots, and finally serving the coffee in a small cup to each guest. This ceremony signifies friendship, hospitality, and Ethiopian culture. This is an ancient culture that Ethiopia still follows, and at every traditional Ethiopian event, you will see a coffee ceremony happening.

One might wonder why coffee is such an integral part of Ethiopian culture. After my arrival in Ethiopia, I was also very keen to know why Ethiopia's coffee ceremony has become such an integral part of its culture. It is like a tea ceremony in Japan. Little did I know at that point that Ethiopia is regarded as the birthplace of coffee and, as a result, has a long and rich history associated with coffee. It is part of the socio-cultural fabric of Ethiopia. It is very important to understand the culture and history of coffee in Ethiopia before you talk about doing anything with the coffee industry.

When we look at coffee, only arabica coffee is grown in Ethiopia. Ethiopia is considered the birthplace of coffee. There is an interesting legend or folklore that is widely believed in Ethiopia. The story of Kaldi, a goat herder This is often told to explain the discovery of coffee. It is widely believed in Ethiopia that the goat herder named Kaldi discovered coffee after seeing its stimulating effects on his goats. The story says that he would take his goats to the forest in Kaffa every day for grazing. In the forest, he found that his goats would become especially energetic after eating berries from a specific tree. As he was unsure about the berries, he took those berries to the local monastery, which termed them a devil's product. The monks in the monastery threw it in the fire, and the aroma of the roasted berries spread across the area. Realizing their mistake, the monks pulled out the berries and smashed them. Then they put it in hot water to preserve it.

The soaking of the smashed beans in the hot water turned the water into a beverage. When they drank it, they also felt energetic, and they claimed that it kept them awake for the midnight devotion. This was the first time coffee was discovered, as per Ethiopian folklore. I don't know if this story is really true or not, and if coffee was actually discovered in Kaffa by KALDI, but the way this story is told, with a lot of pride and belief, and in an exciting manner in Ethiopia, I prefer to believe this story as the real story behind the discovery of coffee. In the later years, the coffee, through the slave trade, reached Yamen and from there to Arabia, and from Arabia, it reached the European and American subcontinents.

Given the fact that there is such an elaborate explanation about how coffee originated in Ethiopia, coffee, since its perceived discovery, has become an integral part of culture in Ethiopia. Any traditional Ethiopian celebration is not complete without a cup of coffee served in the traditional manner. After roasting, grinding, and brewing the coffee for hours together at the traditional Ethiopian coffee celebration, the coffee is offered with popcorn. As this coffee is consumed without any sugar or milk added to it, it is very acidic in nature. Of course, you cannot contaminate the coffee, which is a divine drink anyway, with milk in Ethiopia. For newbies, this coffee creates a lot of acidity, for which popcorn is served as a balance. I had several opportunities to attend coffee ceremonies many times during my stay in Ethiopia, and I must say that the coffee served there is no match to any coffee anywhere in the world that I have ever had. Sometimes, I still miss the Ethiopian coffee and the coffee ceremony, as it used to be a wonderful experience to be part of them.

It is believed that the best coffee in the world is grown in the Yiragachefe area of Ethiopia, which, in the international market, is also an important coffee brand for Ethiopia. Ethiopian coffee is considered special in the world, which is due to the country's varied and diverse agroclimatic conditions and the highlands that give the coffee diverse flavours and profiles. Ethiopia is a significant player in the global coffee market, especially in the arabica coffee segment, and Ethiopian coffee is considered one of the best arabica coffees coming from Africa. However, the value chain of coffee was, at that time, highly skewed in favour of exporters.

The exporters would buy the coffee from the coffee auction centre, located in Addis Ababa, where the coffee aggregators, called akrabis, from all over Ethiopia would bring their coffees for sale. Because it would be offered at an auction, through the auction house, the exporters would look at the coffee lot by lot and then decide.

Once they bought the coffee at the auction from the akrabi, the seller had to transport the coffee to the buyer's warehouse. Once the seller has delivered the coffee to the buyer's warehouse, the exporter or buyer will pay. But it was not so simple. The buyers would write blank checks and avoid payments for several months. In many cases, it takes two to three months for the sellers to be paid.

The Ethiopian economy was import-dependent. The importers would need foreign currency to import the products. The exporters were exporting the coffee to the USA and Europe, creating valuable foreign currency. Most of these exporters were also the biggest importers of the country, as they were the ones with the continuous flow of foreign currency. Once they have the foreign currency in their accounts after export, they will use the foreign currency generated to finance their import business. After the import is done and the product has been sold in the country at a substantial profit, they would then pay the coffee seller his dues.

This meant that the farmer, who was the poorest person on the value chain, would be the biggest financier in the country. It was the farmers who were financing the import business of the large-scale importers in Ethiopia, who were exporting coffee to Europe and America. This value chain was so tightly controlled by the traders that there was absolutely no chance for a farmer to break away and look for a lucrative opportunity elsewhere. In a role reversal, many importers, who were finding it difficult to match the margins of these coffee exporters in the import business, tried to enter the coffee export business to finance their imports. But the value chain was so tightly controlled by the exporters that they never allowed any of these importers to successfully build an export business. In spite of the inefficiencies, the akrabis and the exporter had tight relations, making it difficult for the new exporters to find exportable coffee.

This was an ideal condition for the ECX to accept the government's offer to restructure the trade. The final objective was that the farmers be given an equal opportunity to trade and that the market value chain be structured to bring more balance. This was our biggest opportunity to promote the exchange's relevance, but, for some of us, this was also the biggest risk factor. The coffee business game, as it was actually played, had a lot of unknowns for us. With close to 50% of the country's export earnings coming from coffee, a single wrong step or wrong decision would mean that we would be responsible for a substantial part of the country's revenues. This fact alone was sufficient for many of us to say, let's be cautious about coffee.

CHAPTER EIGHT

COFFEE- THE 90-POUND GORILLA TO BE TAMED

By far, coffee in Ethiopia was the biggest crop in terms of impact. Coffee was one of the major export commodities that Ethiopia had, and roughly 50% of its export revenues were dependent on coffee. The idea of doing anything with coffee was not going to be easy or straight-forward. As we debated about coffee, I was honestly not very aware of what the coffee sector was. Coffee has a long history of production in Ethiopia, and this production can be divided into three categories. It can be plantation coffee, which is a very small percentage of Ethiopian coffee but grown on a large estate on a commercial basis. Then there is garden coffee, which is grown by smallholder farmers along with other crops in the vicinity of their residential area. The third type of production is forest coffee, which is collected from the wildly growing coffee trees in the forest.

Coffee is widely grown in southern and western Ethiopia. It is estimated that coffee is grown in an overall area of four thousand sq. km in Ethiopia. Most of the coffee production is located in the southwestern part of Ethiopia, where Keffa, the birthplace of coffee, is located. The regions where coffee is grown are Yirga Chefe, Sidamo, Harrar, Djimma, and others. Coffee in Ethiopia is grown mainly in the highlands. In Ethiopia, areas with an altitude higher than one thousand meters above sea level are the areas where coffee is grown. The higher the altitude, the better the quality of the coffee. This coffee cultivation in Ethiopia primarily uses traditional methods, and very little mechanization has happened in the coffee sector.

The processing of coffee is done in two ways. It is either sun-dried or washed. Ethiopia uses both sun-dried and wash processing techniques to process its coffee. Most of the processers use the sun-dried method more prominently, whereas the better-quality coffees are the one washed processed in Ethiopia. The sun-dried or natural processing method is a method in which, once the red cherry is ready and picked, it is sorted and less dense cherries are separated. The good cherries, after separation, are taken to a raised bed to be put in sunlight for drying. They are kept in the sun for about twenty one days, after which the cherries are dried. Then, it is milled to remove the husk and stored in the warehouse for final dispatch.

Generally, these raised beds are made of wood and are about waist-high and covered with nylon netting. When the red coffee cherries are put under the sun, the skin and the sticky juice of the cherries dry out because of the sun. During the night, this coffee is covered to protect it from rain, if any. After the process of drying is done, the cherries are then taken to a hulling station, where the outer cherry is removed and the coffee is ready to be packed and dispatched. Sundried processing is a very basic and highly cost-effective method of processing, and as a result, more than 70% of coffee in Ethiopia is processed through this method.

However, close to 30% of the coffee is also processed through washed processing. Under washed processing, the process is more complicated. The red cherries are picked and further sorted by immersion in water. The less dense cherries get separated and float. The good cherries sink. These good cherries are identified and moved to the processing plant. The skin of the cherries is removed by eco-pulpers, which results in parchment coffee. However, after this process, the coffee still has mucilage that needs to be removed. For this, the parchment coffee is kept in the fermentation tank for about two to three days for the mucilage to be removed. After this, the coffee moves to a soaking tank. The coffee remains soaked in these tanks for about twelve hours, and then it is taken to a raised bed where it is dried to the proper moisture level for about two weeks after which the coffee has the right moisture levels . Once the coffee reaches the appropriate moisture level, it is ready to be packed and dispatched.

Between these two processing types, almost all of the coffee in Ethiopia is processed. Once this coffee is processed, it would be sold to the exporters based in Addis Ababa, who will further sell it to international buyers across the world. Ethiopian coffee, because of its distinctive flavour and taste, has a very large international market, which was being catered to by the exporters based in Addis Ababa. However, there were several challenges that the government was facing with the current value chain of coffee and was looking for an alternative to address these challenges. The major challenge that the government was encountering was that most of the coffee vendors were vertically integrated and were able to create a vertical monopolistic chain. The government was keen to break into this chain and ensure that the coffee produced is traded in a more transparent and competitive manner.

The government of Ethiopia had set up elaborate structures for coffee quality testing. These were called the coffee liquoring units. Coffee, as you know, is quality-tested on two parameters. One is the physical examination, or the physical parameters, and the other is the cup test. The cup test is based on the flavour of the coffee and is conducted by qualified professional taster. These are technical experts who taste the coffee and judge it on multiple parameters. Based on international standards, these coffee liquoring units were set up by the government of Ethiopia to evaluate and provide the correct quality parameters for its export coffee.

I was completely ignorant of all these factors until I was pushed into the designing of the structure of coffee trade. Dr. Eleni was pushing hard with the government for coffee to be permitted to be traded at the ECX. This seemed to be an easy way out to keep the exchange relevant and profitable, as the grains were becoming more and more difficult to crack for the exchange. The overall structure of the grain market, as well as the current prevailing prices, made it very difficult for the exchange to sustain grain trading. Prior to this, in June and July 2008, the exchange developed its first strategic plan, and the indications of coffee being traded on the exchange were given in the strategic plan. The strategic plan had very ambitious targets to achieve, and an elaborate strategy to achieve those targets was laid out.

However, all of us knew that replacing a fifty-year-old mechanism of trading, which had been sustained through the communist regime and now the more democratic socialist regime, would be not only difficult but challenging and would put us in a situation where we would have to fight a long battle. However, Dr. Eleni seems quite confident that trading coffee on the exchange would not be as difficult as it seems to be. I believe that by then she had had multiple meetings with policymakers, specifically in the ministry of agriculture and with the deputy prime minister, about coffee. The deputy prime minister was the champion in government for the ECX and was one of its strongest supporters. Dr. Eleni was relying on his support and his help to make the coffee trading permission for Ethiopia's commodity exchange possible.

Eventually, a proclamation was issued by the government of Ethiopia that announced that the structure of coffee trading would be revised, and now, except for those directly happening between farmers and international buyers, every single bean of coffee that is traded in Ethiopia will be traded through the ECX. This was a sudden decision by the government of Ethiopia. However, I personally believe that for the government to arrive at this decision, there was a lot of lobbying done by Dr. Eleni. She worked tearlessly with the government to ensure that the ECX was given the right to trade in coffee. So, in my opinion and my professional judgment, it was not as surprising as it was made out to be by Dr. Eleni. I remember we had a meeting in the evening at the Hilton Hotel on the day when the government announced the new coffee law. Dr. Eleni seemed excited by the proclamation. However, all the other team members were confused and stunned, to say the least. The matter was still being discussed in the management team; however, the willingness of the ECX to accept the offer of the government to launch coffee had already been communicated and accepted by Dr. Eleni.

However, initially, the proclamation did not speak about ECX's exclusivity in the trade. It was also a long-fought battle, after which ECX got the exclusive rights to offer a trading platform for coffee in Ethiopia. The initial proclamation that was issued said that the auction house or the ECX would be allowed to trade coffee. Hence, it meant that the auction system would continue and the ECX would be an alternative.The whole idea of restructuring the coffee trade seems defeated by this, as the coffee trade at the auction was subject to substantial inefficiencies. In such a case, if the auction is allowed to continue, the ECX would not find any traction, and the proclamation as well as the opportunity given to the ECX by it would not be of any use. Later, the government amended the coffee proclamation act, and the ECX was given the exclusive right to trade coffee. This meant that the age-old auction system would be discontinued, the auction centre would be closed, and all the infrastructure available to the auction would be made available to the commodity exchange.

Over the years, I realized that Dr. Eleni had a clear understanding of breaking a current structure into pieces and then selecting the required pieces for her structure to be stronger. This is something she would do very effectively. This was exactly what played out in the coffee sector in Ethiopia. There were a number of key components that were required to be absorbed by the ECX for it to develop the capacity of the coffee trade. One was the warehousing capacity, and the second was the coffee liquoring units.

I remember being told about a story of a heated discussion before the ECX was given the exclusive right to trade coffee. The government of Ethiopia's ministry of agriculture was working on restructuring the coffee trade and addressing the inefficiencies. The new proclamation was already on the cards. However, the modalities were still being worked out. There was a debate between Dr. Eleni and Yacob Yalla, the then state minister for agriculture. At that point, the minister for agriculture was the deputy prime minister, and Yacob was, in all practical matters, responsible for the ministry's work. After a heated discussion with the minister of state, Dr. Eleni is believed to have stormed out of the room, saying either you do it or I do it!

She was in no mood to accept the simultaneous auction and exchange alternative, as was proposed by Yacob. The matter was finally escalated to the DPM's desk, who looked at all the aspects and decided that it was best for the ECX to be the exclusive agency running the trade platform for coffee. He understood that the ECX platform was more transparent, more rule-based, and would be less infiltrated by the exporters, ensuring that the decisions were taken more in the interest of the trade than the interests of the participants. This was a big win for Dr. Eleni, who was vindicated. Her argument was that it should be either the exchange or the auction that runs the trading floor. Both running simultaneously in the coffee sector would not work.

With this, the ball was now in the ECX's court, and we had less than two months to get the coffee trading started. At that point in time, there were a number of questions that we were grappling with. How would the exchange cope with the dramatic increase in trade volumes as our staff and capacities were structured for much less trade? There was also a worry about how the strong exporters lobby would react to this, which had a vested interest in ensuring that the current mechanism of trade continued so that they could continue to benefit as they have in the last fifty years. There was also a worry that the process had to be completed in four months, and we had a very faint idea what coffee was.

Definitely, there were a lot of concerns, but there was also an excitement to address them and champion coffee trading at the ECX. I was one of the very few people in the exchange who had absolutely no idea about the actual taste and importance of coffee. Most of my colleagues at the exchange were Ethiopian diaspora and understood coffee and realized, because of their social awareness, that trading coffee on the exchange is something that is going to be quite challenging. However, I had no such understanding with me and was looking at it more from an objective perspective than any other new commodity. Of course, the fact that it represents close to half of the country's export value was always there, and the pressure because of that was always felt.

The first task I had to achieve was to ensure that the contract specifications for coffee were correctly drafted. This one statement encompasses a huge amount of work that I had to do. I was quite confident that somehow we would overcome this challenge and trade coffee smoothly. We started meeting with the sector's stakeholders to understand the sector. These stakeholders were also trying to understand our thought process on coffee. I remember we used to be very excited and talk to the coffee exporters about how we were going to bring international trading practices into Ethiopia, which would dramatically change the Ethiopian coffee trade. We would talk about how coffee is traded in London and Chicago and emphasize that we will replicate the same trading mechanism in Ethiopia.

I remember one of such meeting with one of the coffee exporters. We were having a one-on-one discussion, stating the same "You know how coffee gets traded in London and Chicago and everywhere in the world. We are building the system that will replicate the best global practices." He was listening to her and then very coolly said, "You guys know how the coffee goes to various parts of the world from Djibouti, but do you have any idea how coffee reaches the Djibouti port from the farmer's backyard? If you don't understand this, you don't know anything about coffee." This statement hit all of us very hard, and we realized that our understanding of coffee was more of the international markets, which was of no use if we did not understand the coffee value chain in Ethiopia.

This was like a wake-up call, and all of us started to spend a lot of time understanding the coffee value chain in Ethiopia. This was the only way for us to address the challenges that this value chain had in domestic circles. By law, in Ethiopia, coffee is an export commodity. Any coffee that pertains to a certain quality has to be compulsorily exported by the trader. However, if the coffee fails to achieve a certain minimum quality standard, it cannot be traded in the domestic market. Unlike any other export commodity, coffee had an equally thriving domestic market. Because of this, there were a lot of times in the year when the export and domestic coffee markets would compete with each other and the sanctity of quality certifications would be compromised. During the discussions, I learned that many times lower-quality beans were assigned to coffee in collusion with the trader by the coffee liquoring unit expert.

This lower-grade coffee meant that the coffee would now be allowed to be traded on the domestic market and may not be compulsorily required to be exported. Many times, especially around festivals, the domestic coffee prices shot up, and in some cases, the domestic prices were more remunerative than the export prices. In such a situation, such things were happening. We were discovering these things as we were gathering more understanding about the coffee value chain in Ethiopia.

As this was going on, Dr. Eleni once called me for a meeting on a Saunday evening. She was at Elephant Café, which was just below my residential apartment. She called me and asked me to come and meet her. I went and met Dr. Eleni in that café. She was pretty convinced that coffee trading would bring a lot of accolades to the exchange and wanted me to lead the contract development exercise. She had some data on her laptop. We started looking at the data and realized that there are a number of origins, which makes it seemingly impossible for standardization to happen. As a concept, standardization was something that was totally alien to the coffee trading community up until now. In the auction process, the coffee was traded based on lots, and every lot, based on its peculiarity, was priced by the buyer. Now, in our system, we were talking about standardizing the quality of the coffee and ensuring that no specific lot-wise identity remains. This was trouble in the making, as I knew.

As Dr. Eleni shared with me the data on coffee trading from the auction centre, and as I went through it, I was not able to understand how I was going to standardize this coffee. I was completely clueless, as the number of origins ran into the thousands. As coffee in Ethiopia is very close to the socio-economic fabric, it is intertwined with the lives of the people, so much so that coffee is named after the village where it is produced, and each village would take pride in naming its coffee after that village name. This meant that as many villages produce coffee, that many varieties or origins of coffee would exist. This was an absolutely crazy thing for an exchange to look at! We could not have contracts for each village and for each location.

However, when we looked at the international market, we realized that there were four to five internationally recognized brands or origins, which were based on the geographical locations in Ethiopia. These were Yiraga Chefe, Sidamo, Harrar, Djimma, and Limu. These four to five brands were internationally recognized. On the production side, there were hundreds of villages that would produce coffee in the geographical areas, which was internationally recognized, but domestically, these coffees were recognized by the village name. As we were working on this, the news spread that we were going to standardize it in four or five groups only. This prompted a lot of concern among the stakeholders, and we used to receive delegations each day from various villages. I remember handling these delegations on a daily basis. They were very concerned about the name of their coffee and would come to us with a lot of complaints and expectations. I would be in these meetings, but, unfortunately, I could not understand what they wanted to tell me. I could not understand amharic. I looked up to my colleague Abenet, and most of the communication was handled by him. Abenet would then explain to me the reason and the complaint they had. I realized that the biggest concern was that each village would come and represent their case for us to not rename their village coffee and retain the name of their village in the coffee identification. This was an indication of how intertwined coffee is in the socio-political and socioeconomic fabric of Ethiopia.

However, this was not possible, and I had to spend a lot of time with the experts from the coffee liquoring unit cracking this standardization. The first thing I had to do was sit with a map and list out which region each producing village pertains to. So, each village was identified as part of a bigger grouping from the four to five groups of geographical location. Once that was done, I had to sit down with the quality experts to understand the minute differences that the agronomic conditions could cause. I tried to understand if, in a blind test of the coffee can, based only on the cup testing parameter, a coffee from a specific village could be identified. The technical expert told us that they can differentiate between major regional coffees but not village by village. Many villages were in the same agronomic belt, which meant that the agronomic specifications of coffee were not very difficult. Based on the agronomic differences in the larger region, we created subgroups. These subgroups, like A, B, and C, for each geographical location were identified, and we grouped the coffee into much more manageable categories.

It is my firm belief, based on what the experts have told me, that this was the best way to do the categorization and standardization. Since then, a lot of publications that I have read over the years have spoken about how wrong our decision was to club these coffees into one major grouping. However, I still believe that the way I structured the coffee contracts into five to six major origins was the best way to address this challenge. It has stood the test of time, and even after many years, it was continuing. This exercise took considerable time for us to develop the groupings and identify each coffee as belonging to one of the identified groupings. Finally, five to six groupings were identified after a detailed discussion with the stakeholders. After the tiring exercise, we had five to six groupings now, with two processing types. Further, each grouping has subgroups. With this, we were down to less than fifty types. These were the final groups that we could zero in on.

Further, based on the physical examination and the cup testing scores of the coffee liquoring units, a quality assessment of the coffees would be done. Before the exchange came into play, the quality parameters were bifurcated into five grades. After the coffee testing, a score would be assigned to it. Based on the score, the coffee would be assigned to one of the five grades. These grades had a very wide range, which meant that anything falling within that range would pertain to that specific quality grade. The coffee technical team advised us that this type of grading is loosely designed and we need to make it more tight. Based on the technical experts' suggestions, we decided to make it more tight by expanding the five grades into ten. The grades were doubled, making them tighter and more specific. This led us to have around forty types and ten grades, making a total of four hundred contracts for coffee. For an exchange, this is a huge number. However, when you consider more than 750 origins x 5 grades, standardizing it into this was an achievement in itself and was not easy.

This required a lot of discussion, negotiation, and spending hours and hours together with the coffee sector stakeholders. I would spend a lot of time with the stakeholders, trying to understand how the detailed quality parameters of coffee were structured. Based on the internationally recognized Ethiopian coffee specifications and origins and the domestic challenges, we had to come up with a balance between the two. And I believe we did a good job. Every day, I and my colleague, Abenet, would go to different stakeholders, have meetings and discussions with them, and take their views to ensure that whatever we did was based on sound research.

As a mark of respect towards the visiting guest, every coffee trader would offer us a small shot of coffee, which would be served without milk or sugar. Adding sugar or milk to the coffee is considered an insult to the taste of coffee, and as the Arabs are respectful towards their tea, the Ethiopians are equally respectful towards their coffee. To build rapport with the stakeholders, I had to drink that cup of coffee at every meeting. Finally, in three to four days, I realized that so much of the strong Ethiopian coffee was making my stomach highly acidic, and I would have to skip my dinner because of the hyperacidity that this coffee was creating. Mind you, I was an Indian, and for me, coffee was instant coffee. Abenet, realizing the problem, gives me a solution. He suggested that I should rather ask for tea, so that nobody feels bad and I am also able to manage it easily. As it is, the host would ask us, "Shay-Buna?" , meaning tea or coffee? I switched my strategy, and it worked.

By early September, we were done with the contract specification for coffee. The biggest challenge was the coffee quality parameters as well as the classification of coffee. We had addressed both challenges, and when I presented this, it was well appreciated and accepted by the team. When I was working tirelessly on developing these contract specifications, everybody else was working on their own set of challenges. Ben had a challenge about how to bring in all the akrabis into the system. The akrabis is the name given to the aggregators of coffee, who normally buy coffee from their village farmers, aggregate it, and sell it to the coffee buyers at the auction. These akrabis were the major component of the market, and they were thousands in number.

When the idea of a commodity exchange was floated, the biggest challenge was how an akrabi could become a member. Initially, we suggested a solution: an akrabi could be a client and trade through a member of the exchange. This was the conventional exchange structure. However, this was very quickly shot down, as this meant that the akrabis had to disclose details and depend for their trade on somebody else. This was not possible, as they would like to negotiate the deal themselves, then give out the price and suggest the trade. There was a lot of distrust in the coffee market, and because the coffee trade was done in a very close circle, people were not willing to offer or share their trading prices or strategies with anybody else.

When we reached a deadlock and Ben had to find a way to add the akrabis as members, he came up with an innovative solution, suggesting that we should add a new category of members, which would be only selling members. In any case, akrabis were the traders who would only sell and not buy from the exchange. The market has a well-defined role for them: to sell the coffee, as the law identified the buyers and the sellers as distinct. The law made it mandatory for buyers to have registration with the government, and only exporters would be authorized to buy, meaning that an akrabi would never be allowed to buy. The same way, the buyers would only be buyers and not sellers anymore. Based on this legal bifurcation between buyers and sellers, we could introduce a new category of membership with lower capital requirements. This was the limited right to membership that had been worked out as a wonderful solution to the issue. These limited buyers were buy-only members and sell-only members. These, in hundreds of numbers, were added to the system.

At that time, there were hundreds of traders who were trying to get into the coffee trade too. The coffee was dominated by a very small number of buyers—less than fifteen—who would control more than the majority of the market. Still, the market had a number of small buyers, and each one of them had to be accommodated in the new system. For this reason, the concept of buying and selling members with limited rights was considered a wonderful innovation, and we included these changes in our system.

The biggest challenge that faced us was how we were going to develop a system that would accommodate all the coffee that is produced in the country and be warehoused. Our warehousing capacities were limited. This was addressed as the government made available various warehouses in regional and rural locations where the coffee was grown. These warehouses had to be equipped, however, to the standards of the exchange, and proper networking had to be done, as the ECX worked on an electronic mechanism of networking. Under the mechanism, each warehouse would have a computer system that would be linked to the central depository database in Addis Ababa. Every deposit of the day would be updated in the central depository, which would then issue the warehouse receipts. This meant that every new warehouse required networking and systems to be installed. In addition, the process of receiving coffee quality certification and storage was to be addressed during the first phase.

That time, we did not have an officer heading the warehousing, and Ahadu was assigned the responsibility of looking after the warehousing systems. Solomon was also assisting him, as a major component of making the warehouses ready was related to technology development. Eventually, we were able to add several warehouses into the system and match up with the expectation of having all these warehouses ready for deposits. IT systems were installed and the warehouses were made ready in the initial four months. Solomon was not only having a challenge ensuring that the hardware installation at the warehouse happened but also the network connectivity, as a lot of these warehouses were in areas where the internet was not that easily available. In 2008/2009, Ethiopia did not have the spread of the internet as it does today, and in such an environment, making these warehouses operational in rural locations was definitely a challenge. Solomon was able to use the dongles for internet connectivity, and with multiple redundancies, he was able to structure a network of the warehouses where these warehouses could dump their data into the exchange central depository system either in real-time or in batches.

One of the key aspects that we were highlighting as our USP was that we would demonstrate the prices of New York coffee trading in the exchange trading floor. Till then, the practice used to be that once a week, the auction centre would disclose the prices on the New York Exchange, and then those prices continued to be posted for seven days. However, since the commodity exchange trading floor was equipped with price display boards, along with such price display boards being deployed across the country, it was critical that these price display boards get the right information at the right time to be displayed. This challenge was addressed by Aahdu, who developed a mechanism for collecting the prices from the international markets on a real-time basis and displaying them on the floor of the exchange. This was definitely a game-changer for the akrabis, who now realized that they could have the same price information as the exporters or the buyers. Developing the rules in line with the coffee proclamation for the exchange was done by Yohannes, and we were all set to trade at the end of November 2008.

CHAPTER NINE

COFFEE IS FINALLY BREWING

On November 26, 2008, I was at the Sheraton Hotel to celebrate the launch of coffee at the ECX. It was the formal announcement of the launch of coffee trading at the ECX. We were having a good time after four months of hard work. I was totally oblivious to the situations in Mumbai that were unfolding. It was only the next morning, when I and Yohannes entered the office together, that he asked me, "Hi Bharat, is your family okay?" I said yes; I just dropped them off at their schools. He then asked if in India everything was okay. I said, "Yes, what happened? Why are you asking it?" He replied, "You didn't see the news? They have blown up the Taj Mahal!" The first thought that came to mind was that a terrorist attack or a bomb explosion had damaged the Taj Mahal in Agra. However, I quickly logged onto the internet to check what had happened. Almost immediately, I froze as I saw the images of terrorist attacks happening in Mumbai. I called a few friends to check that everybody in Mumbai was okay, and I realized that it was an unprecedented attack happening and still undergoing in Mumbai.

Coming back to coffee, the day the launch function of the coffee trading was held was an important day for us. The day we met in the Hilton hotel four months ago to learn that coffee trading will shift to the ECX, and today, at the Sheraton, where we were confident that now we have these structures in place to accommodate the coffee trading, we had virtually crossed the bridge. It was a very difficult four months for us, and we were in complete start-up mode to ensure that we were ready by the end of November and did not miss the coffee session starting in December. During this period, multiple sessions of interactions with various stakeholders happened, and we developed very tight quality standards for the identified classification of coffee. Warehouse, market data, technology platform—everything got a serious capacity lift, and we were now ready to have a tenfold increase in our volumes. The staff strength had significantly increased, and all the departments had almost doubled their capacities in terms of staff. We had added close to four hundred new members to the system, and that too at a very affordable price. All in all, we were now ready to trade in coffee.

Before we finalized the specifications, another issue that was facing us was the loss of moisture. Because coffee, over time in storage, would lose moisture, and as a result, the weight would go down. The exchange was faced with a situation where the coffee was stored for a certain period, which meant that the coffee had reduced in the exchange warehouses. Here we understood that sometimes coffee "disappears" from the warehouse, and moisture loss is blamed for it. We had to address this issue. On discussion, a technical expert suggested that there should be a fixed deduction that should be adjusted for each deposit. But how much the fixed deduction should be was not something that was easy to decide. Ultimately, as this was a risk issue, the chief Risk Officer of the exchange, Dr. Kadri Alfah, decided to do a scientific study. He measured the actual moisture loss by keeping the sample coffee in the warehouse and measuring the moisture loss at regular intervals. Eventually, based on this scientific study, where he measured the moisture loss per week and calculated how much loss needs to be adjusted based on the storage time, With this calculation, the levels of deduction to be applied were adopted by the exchange. This was the first time that the exchange had actually taken into account a more structured manner of moisture loss calculations.

Ethiopia in 2008 had a very controlled economy, with the government controlling the country with an iron fist. Going against the government was not an option, as there was virtually no political opposition in Ethiopia. I remember a story from the 2009 elections. During the run-up to the elections, the government ensured that its popularity outshone the opposition. A friend of mine used to run a factory for packaging materials used by flower exporters. He told me that once one of the drivers of a flower farm, who used to come to pick up the packing material, came and gave a flower to one of his female workers. This caused a fight between two female workers for some reason. My friend, in order to manage the situation, fired the workers for indiscipline. These workers reached out to the local labour office, and labour inspectors visited my friend. When he told them about the flower incident, they said it is good that you have fired them because giving and taking flowers is considered a crime as the flower is an opposition election symbol!

Ethiopia was a country with a very strong government. In such a case, when the commodity exchange was being discussed for coffee and we were preparing for our trade, nobody very openly opposed us. We did not hear or see any type of reservation about the exchange. Even the exporters did not show any kind of opposition to the government's move to introduce the ECX as the coffee exchange. However, as the coffee trading was launched, we had an unexpected onslaught from the coffee traders, particularly the international buyers. The international media and the international buyers, who were renowned global giants in coffee, started accusing Ethiopia and the government of Ethiopia of damaging the coffee trade. They even gave out a verdict that the exchange in coffee trading would lead to a reduction of coffee exports.

I remember speaking to a very agitated global head of quality for Starbucks. He was very angry at the Ethiopian government and the ECX. He had come into our office to try to understand the quality and classification that we had developed. I was doing my best to explain to him why these classifications had been made. However, he was in no mood to listen and was accusing us of killing the coffee trade in Ethiopia. Though initially I tried to explain to him the reason why we were doing so, eventually, realizing that it was falling on deaf ears, I stopped my effort to convince him. I think he had a genuine worry that his business, which was heavily dependent on getting a specific blend from Ethiopia, might be disturbed. Because of the ECX coming into play, one of the things that was going to happen was no preservation of the coffee based on the identity of the depositor. The coffee was preserved based on the grades and commingled with the similar grades in the warehouse. This implies that if the coffee is grade one of Djimma origin, then all the coffee with grade one of Djimma origin will be stored together making it absolutely impossible to identify the sack or the deposit that a specific depositor had deposited. This was considered losing traceability, and the argument put forward by a lot of international coffee buyers was that this would lead to the commoditization of coffee. They further said that Ethiopia is earning premiums in international markets because of its specialty coffee.

For me, in honesty, I was also clueless on what is a specialty coffee? Nobody could define it for me. When I asked even the international buyers what they define as specialty coffee, they said it's a special blend of coffee. But what exactly? At least I was not able to understand. In fact, I was not from a coffee background, so understanding the technical aspects of specialty coffee was all the more difficult. We were accused that by introducing a mechanism for exchange trading, we had killed specialty coffee brands, and now we are going to get lesser prizes for our coffees. That would be a disaster for thc market. This was the first time that we realized that building structures and getting internal readiness was not enough. We had to work very hard to ensure that the international buyers were on our side and that they were supporting the initiative of the ECX, which was nowhere to be seen.

The international buyers were worried that their specific blend would be lost and that they might find it difficult to maintain the same blend for their roasting. Up until now, because of the virtual vertical integration, a lot of these buyers were buying based on the identity of the supplier and not the quality of the coffee. This meant that, in a way, they were ensuring that the coffee came from the same farm year after year. This was set to change, as even the akrabis would not know whose sack was delivered to the buyer. The trade would happen with an individual; however, the delivery would not be of the same sack that the depositor had deposited. This was the biggest bone of contention throughout the first year. In the initial days of trading, we started to see some volumes, but as the trading days passed, we started to realize that the buyers are buying the minimum quantity, that they could, and that we are not in a position to convince the buyers, as they claimed that the international market has reduced the consumption of Ethiopian coffee. Because they do not have any orders from the international market, their buying capacity is also limited.

But from the akrabis' side, they were loving the new system. They felt they were given more power in the trade. I remember when the exchange started, on the first day of coffee trading, we had a sixty-year-old akrabi on the floor. This guy was very excited, and his body language showed that he was enjoying the opportunity he was given by the ECX. As the bids and offers started to flow, he was very loud and very strong in his quoting of prices. When the deal happened, he was very happy, and after the trading session was over, he came to me and Abenet, and started speaking. I could make out he was thanking us in Amharic. He seemed to be very emotional and talking about a lot of things. I was, unfortunately, not getting a clue of what he wanted to say, as I could not understand Amharic. Later on, when I asked Abenet about what he meant, Abenet told me that he was very happy and was thanking the ECX for giving him the opportunity to offer prices to the buyer, which he had never done before. He also said that he has been trading in coffee for the last forty years, and never in his life did he think that he would be able to offer prices on an equal footing to the buyer and would be able to negotiate the prices with the buyer, as he has done today.

This was an entirely new day, and a new mechanism was working for him. He was obviously enjoying the exchange system. The people who are happy with the exchange system are the akrabis, or aggregators, who are coming to the exchange and getting better prices than the auction platform. On the auction platform, they were more or less voiceless, whereas at the ECX, they were given equal power to negotiate the prices as the exporter would have. Since that day, a lot of akrabis have come and thanked us. These akrabis at that time, who were barely able to read and write, somehow learned to write the ticket for them. Even in some cases, we allowed ticket writers to write the tickets, as the akrabis were completely illiterate. But they demonstrated a wonderful trading mindset and were making the most of the opportunity that was offered to them.

However, on the buy side and in the international market, there was a lot of negative media going around, making it difficult for the ECX. The Ethiopian government was also keeping tabs on all the developments and trying to understand where the opposition was coming from. Once Dr. Eleni was in the United States to address a coffee sector meeting, she was booed and was not allowed to even speak by the buyers from America and Europe. They were very angry with the exchange and voiced their anger against the Ethiopian government and specifically the ECX in very strong terms. Definitely, Dr. Eleni was not prepared for this, as this was the first time in her career that she was countered by such an aggressive crowd. I remember how much that incident shook her up and had an impact on all of us.

We realized that this needs to be countered, and to ensure that the buyers come back to ECX in a more satisfied manner, we started to have a very strong representation about the benefits of the exchange and how it is bringing sanctity into the market. We also showed a lot of flexibility by offering to make a lot of structural changes. This outreach by the ECX started to work in the exchange's favour. As we were slowly winning the trust of the buyers, another major setback jolted the exchange. The Ethiopian government was patiently looking at the situation and was telling the buyers not to boycott the exchange and to continue buying and earning export revenues for the country.

The Ethiopian government realized that some of the large exporters were trying to hold Ethiopia for ransom by not trading on the exchange and making it look like international buyers were not interested in buying from Ethiopia. The government identified that several exporters from Ethiopia had a standing contract to supply coffee, and they were defaulting on their international contracts because they wanted to put the blame on the ECX. They were not ready to buy from the Exchange. The prime minister and other ministers had repeatedly issued veiled warnings to the exporters against boycotting the Exchange. Eventually, in June 2009, a drastic step was taken by the government.

That morning I was driving to the ECX when my driver, who was listening to the radio news, suddenly said, "My god! Did you listen to that?" The news was running on the radio in the car, but since it did not know Amharic, I could not gather much of it. He explained to me that the government has announced that, on the instructions of the Prime Minister, it has decided to crack down on the exporters who are not fulfilling their orders in the international market. As per the government, by doing so, they are threatening the national security of Ethiopia. Because they are defaulting on their international contracts, the foreign currency that should be flowing into the country, necessary for the country to buy essential medicines and other supplies, is getting affected. As a result, the government has decided to hold them responsible and take appropriate action against them. Finally, after reaching the office, I realized that some exporters had been arrested and placed behind bars, with all their coffee in the warehouses being confiscated by the government. These exporters had bought coffee from the exchange also, but had not picked it up from the exchange warehouse. The coffee was still in the exchange warehouse. It was estimated by us that about seventeen thousand tons of coffee were confiscated by the government, and it was decided that this coffee would be sold off by the government at the exchange platform, which meant that the same coffee would be reclaimed on the exchange platform. This was something we were not ready for.

As per the government rule, no coffee would be re-traded. It meant that once the coffee has been traded and the warehouse receipt has been transferred from the seller to the buyer, that warehouse receipt cannot be offered for re-trade. However, in this case, because of the government directive, we had to create a bypass to the structure, where the buyer can now again sell the same warehouse receipt. It was decided that the government would use EGTE to sell the coffee that it had confiscated from the exporters. As this was going on, we were struggling to identify the exchange rules and the regulatory authority's regulations in this regard. As an exchange, we were standing in trust towards the members for the coffee that they had procured from the exchange platform. All the coffee that the exporters had procured was in our custody on behalf of the exporters. Since this was a government crackdown, the minister called us and told us to hand over all the coffee that belongs to these exporters to the government.

We had a big debate on this and unanimously decided that it could not be accepted. Yohannes, our compliance head, was very clear that the coffee is deposited in the exchange warehouse and held by the exchange in trust for the exporter. In the absence of any legitimate legal document directing the exchange to transfer ownership to the government, the exchange is not entitled to hand over and should not be handing over the coffee to the government. When the exchange's point of view was communicated to the government, the minister was not amused, and a debate between the then minister of state, Yacob Yalla, and Yohannes in his office happened. Yacob was very agitated and wanted the exchange to hand over all the coffee on his orders to the EGTE. However, Yohannes stood his ground, stating that, in the absence of a court order directing the exchange to hand over the coffee, The exchange is mandated not to do so. If the government is interested in confiscating that coffee, it should ask the court to issue an order in that regard.

Yacob had no time for this and was never used to such pushback from any agency in Ethiopia. He was not understanding why an exchange would need a court order when the government had decided to do so. That was the way business in Ethiopia used to be. The irritation of Yacob went to a level where he even threatened Yohannes to put him and the whole team members of the exchange behind bars if they did not comply. Yohannes stood his ground and said he may do so, but ECX will not be bullied by the government in this manner. Again, the matter landed up on the deputy PM's desk, who eventually asked the ministry to write a formal notice to the ECX, which will ask the ECX to hand over the coffee. Doing so, based on this notice, was not agreed upon by Yohannes, but Dr. Eleni decided to hand over the coffee to the government. With this, all the coffee that was held in the exchange warehouse was handed over to the government, which used the EGTE to offload it in the market again. The money that was received was paid to the exporters after they were released from jail as well. But what this did was bring in a lot of distrust. All the efforts to win over the buyers have now gone to waste for the ECX.

I was always of the opinion that the Exchange should not mandate any commodity for trade on its platform. If an exchange gets a compulsory mandate for a commodity, it will lose out on the perception of the participants. The participants do not see the value of the exchange, as they are forced to trade on it. As a result, in the case of commodities that are not mandated, exchanges find it difficult to create a market. Such commodities do not have a market on the exchange because participants are not interested. My apprehension came through, as after three to four years, when we looked at the exchange composition of trade, we found that only mandatory commodities were making up more than 99% of the trade.

In preparation for the trade, a new concept was introduced. Initially, it was in discussion but could not be implemented at the time of launch. Now we have introduced a new system of trade uniforms. The authorized representatives were issued jackets, which were of distinct colours based on their roles. The buyers were given khaki jackets, which had a close resemblance to gold and represented the buyer, and the sellers were given green jackets, which represented the commodity. On the jackets, their registration numbers were also printed, and they were mandated to wear these jackets while trading. I remember me and Abenet going to the mercato, which was the biggest market in Ethiopia, to look for the cloth with matching colours and getting the jacket stitched. This whole thing—the cloth procurement, stitching, and printing of the numbers on the jackets—was to be done before launch. Before the trading in coffee began, these jackets were ready and distributed to the representatives. These jackets brought a different kind of aesthetic to the trading floor, and certainly the trading floor started to look very professional and very lively. This was one of many contributions that I made to the ECX trading floor.

There were some interesting aspects that came up when we were designing the contract specification for the coffee. One of the interesting aspects that we realized was that the exporters would deduct a huge percentage from the payment to the seller as the deduction for parchment. The coffee came with parchment, and the seller was paid close to twenty percent below the price as a deduction for parchment. There was no scientific reason to prove that the parchment was a certain percentage of the overall weight. When the contract specification at the exchange was launched, the deduction of parchment was not allowed, which meant that the buyers had to pay more. This was a problem the buyers had with the contract specifications. They pointed out that they need the prices to be adjusted for the parchment, and based on the existing parchment deduction system, the deduction should be calculated. However, we explained to them that when they decide the price, they should include this parchment adjustment issue and quote a price that adjusts the parchment. From our end, we would not have a separate deduction for the parchment. Finally, that was understood by the buyers, and the deduction for the parchment was removed from the coffee trade.

Eventually, the exchange reach-out mechanism, the government's iron fist, and the overall acceptance by the akrabis made the resistance slowly fade away. This was the time when the ECX also partnered with the Specialty Coffee Association of America (SCAA) and worked very closely to develop the world's first specialty coffee auction. As this was conducted by the exchange, it was a particularly interesting concept that we had introduced. The top-quality grades of the coffee were selected as specialty coffee, and those coffees were offered for trade in the specialty coffee segment. The auction for specialty coffee was an identity-based transaction, similar to the auction carried out earlier. The quality specifications of the coffee parameters would be highlighted, and the buyers could look at the catalogue, which described the quality and other specifications. Based on that catalogue, the buyers would offer their prices for that specific lot. This was all done online, and a separate system was designed for this.

This was again a way for the ECX to show its outreach to specialty coffee buyers and its willingness to go beyond the normal call of duty to make these buyers comfortable in the exchange. As time passed, the ECX settled down in the coffee trade, though it took about a year for the ECX to settle down. Now, by the late 2009, with coffee well under control, it was time to look at more commodities, and sesame was the next one to be looked into.

Dr Bharat Kulkarni with the trainees at the Ethiopia Commodity Exchange project in June2007

ECX Trading Floor in 2008

ECX Senior Management Team in 2009;

From Right to Left- Mr. Yonas, Mr. Ahadu Woubshet, Dr. Eleni Gabreemadhin, Dr Kadri Alfah (Back), Mr Bemnet Aschenaki (front) , Dr Bharat Kulkarni (Author) and Mr Solomon Eddosa

Photo Courtesy- Ethiopia Commodity Exchange Photographer

Author with his Team at Langano in 2009;

From Right to Left- Mr. Makruia, Mr. Fekadu, Dr. Bharat Kulkarni (Author), Mr. Samson, and Mr Abenet Bekele

Photo Courtesy- Ethiopia Commodity Exchange Photographer

Author with H.E. Jakaya Mrisho Kikwete at World Economic Forum in 2011. ;

The Economic Times on Sunday MAY 8, 2011 23 global indians

Brain Behind E Africa's First Commodity Exchange

Bharat Kulkarni helped Ethiopia wake up and smell the coffee. Now other African countries are following the lead

:: Ishani Duttagupta

His business card says chief economist of Ethiopia Commodity Exchange. But Bharat Kulkarni's role in creating the exchange–the first one in east Africa– has been a much bigger one. He joined the United Nations wing UNDP in 2008 with the job of advising the Ethiopian government in setting up the trading operations of the exchange. "This is the only commodities exchange in east Africa and I was involved in setting it up. Till late last year, I was head of operations and now my role has been extended to research activities and to share our experience with other African governments in the region," says Kulkarni, who is a PhD in Economics, with an MBA in finance from Indore.

It all started in 2007, when as an employee of Multi Commodity Exchange in Mumbai, Kulkarni was a part of the team that advised the Ethiopian government on the commodities exchange. After a couple of visits to the Ethiopian capital Addis Ababa, when he was involved in training and consultancy for the exchange, Kulkarni landed with a job offer that was too good to refuse. "The challenge in setting up the exchange was just what I needed. The terms of employment too were very attractive because I was to be an employee of a United Nations body," he recalls.

Besides his role in running operations, Kulkarni has also advised the ECX management on different issues ranging from trading, risk management, clearing and settlement to acquiring electronic trading technology under World Bank procurement. And as head of trading operations, he designed the world's first exchange-based trading platform for speciality coffee, of which Ethiopia is among the world's largest producers–an achievement that he's very proud of.

"ECX is the first of its kind in Africa. It is a marketplace which serves the various stakeholders, including farmers, traders, processors, exporters and consumers. It was set up by the government to serve coffee growers since the country is among the largest producers of coffee. The other commodities traded on the exchange are sesame seeds and pea-beans. Only physical spot trades are carried out on the exchange on a daily basis," says Kulkarni, who is very proud of the fact that after the exchange was set up, 78% of the total value of sesame exports now go into the pockets of the farmers. He adds that the exchange flawlessly handles an average trade of over $7 mn a day.

Besides coffee, sesame seeds and pea-beans are also traded. The exchange handles trade worth $7 mn on an average

Kulkarni, who started his career as a commodities trader in India, moved to Ethiopia in 2008 and is now very comfortable about living and working in Africa. "Ethiopia doesn't have a colonial history and hence there's no racism. Unlike other East African countries, the Indian community is not very big in Ethiopia–there has been a small trickle of Gujarati businessmen who came to Addis Ababa and other cities from neighbouring countries. But Indian professionals are very well respected here," he says.

According to Kulkarni, Indian professionals are more comfortable in Ethiopia than in neighbouring countries such as Kenya or Tanzania. "Ethiopia is safer and more secure and politically more stable. The local people are friendlier towards expat Indians and more and more Indian companies are investing in Ethiopia in sectors such as manufacturing and agro-industries. With more investment coming in from India, the number of Indian professionals too are increasing," he adds.

Kulkarni's wife Runa is a teacher in a school in Addis Ababa and their five-year-old daughter has just joined an international school. "We feel very safe living in Ethiopia and professionally ECX has been a very challenging assignment," Kulkarni says. But that hasn't stopped him from remaining engaged with academic pursuits and delivering lectures on topics close to his heart.

INDIA CONNECT

- Indian professionals feel safer in Ethiopia than in neighbouring Kenya or Tanzania because there is no history of racism and the country is more stable politically
- Indian companies investing in Ethiopia are mainly in manufacturing and agro-industries

NRI CENTRE

(Do you have an immigration related question? Our experts provide the solutions)

Rami Fakhoury
Fakhoury Law Group, PC, Troy, Michigan

Q Why is the recent Iowa H-1B criminal prosecution significant?

Sujata Malik, San Francisco

A In the Iowa case, lawyers for the US department of justice and the defendant, Vision Systems Group–a now defunct New Jersey IT staffing firm, and three of its executives–agreed to accept a guilty plea of one count of felony wire fraud. By accepting a plea of guilty, the defendants avoided the threat of long prison sentences and large personal fines. The court dropped nine additional charges. VSG had argued that the company's practices were consistent with existing US law, and its lawyers filings said this prosecution was really a part of a larger quarrel over immigration policy.

For more questions and answers on immigration go to www.experts.economictimes.com

Article in The Economic Times edition of 8th May 2011 about Author.

CHAPTER TEN

The Billion Dollar Club

In the first six to eight months of 2009, coffee occupied everything, and every major activity at the ECX revolved around coffee. On one hand, we were struggling and fighting to get our internal systems right, but at the same time, there was a perception battle that we had to fight. With the perception that the government wants to take over the coffee trade, the introduction of the exchange was opposed by European and American buyers. However, as time passed and we started responding effectively to the opposition of the ECX, the opposition started to subside and people started to adjust to the new way of life in coffee. People realized that the exchange is something that is here to stay, and they need to adjust to the new market structure rather than trying to fight it.

There were some astute traders who recognized this at the outset and concentrated their efforts on getting as much traction at the exchange as possible in the early days. As a result, they were able to gain a foothold in the coffee trade while the big boys kept coming up with excuses to avoid trading at the exchange. I recall an extremely intriguing event that occurred at the ECX in the early days, probably on the first or second day of trading. At the time, the systems at the exchange were different from how people were used to trading at the auction, where buyers were not worried about how much they were purchasing because they were not paying upfront in that system. Nevertheless, when they came to the ECX, they were allowed to trade only up to the level of deposits that they had in their settlement bank accounts. Every morning, the exchange clearing and settlement manager would electronically request the information from the bank for all the settlement accounts. This would tell the exchange about the deposits made by each of the buying members. This system was introduced to ensure that no one buys in excess to the deposit, and we are faced with the situation where there are defaults related to trade. In other words, whatever you buy, the money should already be deposited in the bank account, and the exchange could use that money to settle the trade. This ensured that the exchange was able to settle all the trades at the end of the day. On may call it as 100% margins.

As the exchange started trading, one of the biggest coffee trader's representatives, who was also his son, was in the trading floor. He was one of the few big exporters who, right from day one, started participating on the exchange platform. The trading started to happen, and the bids and offers were flowing on the trading floor. He started buying and ended up buying quantities that were much bigger than the deposits he had. This meant that the trades above and beyond his deposit limits were rejected. Immediately after the session, he was told that his trades were rejected as there was no money. He felt offended and very disturbed, as he considered this a loss of his pride in the market. He said to us "What will happen if people come to know that I don't have money to buy coffee". He further offered us that he has money in his office in cash, which he can immediately bring, and requested that we take that money and allow the trade to be approved.

We tried to explain to him that this was not possible as the exchange works only on banking transfers and cash acceptance is not in our model. I knew this was not what he wanted to hear. He was pleading and requesting that we get his limits enhanced, which would allow him to trade beyond his limits. This was his first experience with the exchange, and the processes had not sunk in with him. As a result, he was confused about why and how the trade could be rejected. Eventually he learned the tricks of the trade and started to keep an eye on the balances and ensure that his trades were within the deposit balances. But that experience was an interesting one, teaching us how difficult it would be for the market to adapt to the new system and be part of the exchange trading system.

It is not only traders who are facing this challenge. Even the staff at the commodity exchange and the depositors were learning the new system every day. Even as senior management, we were in a learning mode and trying to understand and learn new things every day as new challenges kept coming to us. Another interesting story I remember here is about a deposit coming into one of the rural warehouses. As per the requirements of the government regulations, we opened warehouses across Ethiopia, and many of these warehouses were located in areas that were very rural and did not have a lot of infrastructure. However, credit goes to Solomon and his team for ensuring that any location where the warehouse is opened was equipped with the electronic system, which was made up of a basic computer and an internet connection for data transmission, which was the lifeline for the warehouse. Every piece of data that is recorded by the exchange warehouse computer was to be transmitted to the head office every day without fail, and by far, the system was working fine. The application developed by the technology team required a lot of information to be recorded in order to identify the depositor and create an audit trail for the deposit. This information, apart from the basic information about the name and address of the depositor, also included details like transport information, including the truck registration plate. Unless and until the driver's license details and the truck registration plate number were recorded, the system would not permit the recording of the deposits.

Solomon's team had gone to all the rural locations and, after installing these computers, rigorously trained the staff there to use them and ensure that minimal data entry errors were recorded on a real-time basis. There was a hotline between Solomon and each warehouse to ensure that any technical glitch was immediately addressed. Solomon and his team members were confident that the system would not encounter any technical glitches to be reported from the warehouse, and if they did, it would be readily addressed. Solomon had thought through all the contingencies that could arise and had planned for them in his action plan. However, it is a fact that you cannot plan for all the contingencies, and sometimes you're caught up in a situation that you never anticipated. We also experienced the same thing just a few days after the coffee deposits in the exchange warehouse started.

That day, Solomon received a call from one of the rural warehouses. The caller was the warehouse manager of a warehouse in a rural location and seemed to be a bit stressed. He called Solomon and told him that there was an IT problem, because of which he was not able to accept the deposit in the warehouse. Solomon immediately, in alert mode, started asking the questions to identify the problem. When Solomon asked about the reason, he was more confused. Solomon asked, "Is the computer working? Is the application working? Is the power on?" Everything was a yes. Now Solomon was confused because all the contingencies that could arise had been confirmed and nothing of that contingency existed. When Solomon inquired what exactly was the problem, the warehouse manager told him, "I am unable to record the deposit and move to the next page." Solomon asked him to explain the exact problem he's facing, and the warehouse manager on the other side said, "Without entering the truck registration plate number, this system is not allowing me to move forward. I want to bypass the truck registration plate number details."

Solomon could not understand and asked him why he wanted to do so, as that is mandatory information that has to be collected. The warehouse manager on the other side was unable to understand why Solomon was being so unreasonable and told him again that he would not be in a position to record the truck plate number. When Solomon tried to know more, the warehouse manager informed him that the deposits had not come in the truck, so there was no truck to record the information. More confused, Solomon asked him how the deposit could arrive without a truck. He said, "Sir, the deposit has come on donkey back!! Unfortunately, we had no system for recording a donkey number into the system. This was a contingency that Solomon had never planned for or even imagined. Now, after all the systems had been tested and gone live, Solomon had the faintest idea how to address this problem. I used to sit next to him, and he reached out to me to inform me about this problem. First, I was also confused, but then I brainstormed and found it really difficult to address this problem.

By law, once the coffee has reached the exchange warehouse, it cannot be turned back, as the coffee proclamation stated. Now we are faced with the situation where there is a deposit to be accepted mandatorily, and our systems are unable to process or record the information. We brainstormed and finally decided that a manual record of the donkeys would be maintained, and in the plate number, the donkey identification number, as per the manual records, would be put in. This incident was both funny as well as stressful, as it taught us a very important lesson: in a market like Ethiopia, there are many factors that we take for granted that may not be a reality. Even very basic things may not work out the same way.

However, the hallmark of our project in Ethiopia was that we always faced situations that we never anticipated and came out of such situations with very innovative solutions. This was the reason we were able to stabilize coffee trading on the exchange, despite challenges from all sides. The coffee experience was definitely a learning experience, as we learned a lot of things about structuring the markets, which involved a large sector of society as stakeholders. The real biggest lesson that I learned is that an exchange has to be highly responsive and flexible in its approach. The exchange is for the market, not the other way around, and if the exchange is not able to understand and adapt to market demands, the relevance of the exchange will quickly fade. This learning was then inbuilt into our philosophy as we moved to other commodities, including sesame.

With the whole 2008/2009 crop year spent on stabilizing coffee and nothing else, with the beginning of the 2009 crop year, we started to look at sesame and identified sesame and white pea beans as the next set of commodities to be traded on the exchange. For planning about sesame, we were more organized and prepared in our approach, something that we had learned from coffee. We knew the challenges that would arise and were well prepared to address those challenges. This was a more organized approach towards sesame and white pea beans and made the introduction of sesame and white pea beans comparatively easy and smooth at the exchange. Honestly, it was not only our effort but also the industry structure that played a role in making sesame and white pea beans both work. Both were primarily exported commodities and unlike coffee, did not have a very large domestic market. This meant that the value chain was much simpler and easier to restructure for them. The sesame and white pea beans had a more structured form of quality specification, which meant that the subjective quality parameters like that in coffee were not present in the sesame or white pea beans. It was purely its physical characteristics, which could be easily defined objectively, that made up the quality specifications.

Thirdly, sesame and white beans were both commodity crops, which meant that they were traded in bulk and that lot or origin identity was not important for the buyers of sesame. They would buy bulk quantities and put the supplies into processing in their factories in China or Europe, as the case may be. These things made us more comfortable with sesame and white pea beans, and we started working on their introduction into the exchange. By this time, the volume of coffee trading was also picking up, and we had introduced even the reject coffee, as it was known. The rejected coffee was tradable for the domestic market, as I had explained earlier. The coffee qualifying for the minimum quality specifications was to be exported, and anything that is rejected for export can only be traded in the domestic market. Since coffee had a single market in the country, which was the ECX, we had to start trading in domestic coffee as well. This trade started to pick up as we moved into the financial year 2009. By this time, the exchange was getting settled, and our revenues were increasing.

In 2008/2009, the value of the trade at the exchange was just around 300 million dollars. As the business improved and we moved into the 2009/2010 financial year, we touched a trade value in excess of 500 million dollars. This was primarily because coffee values were increasing and new commodities were being added. It was in June 2010 that the proclamation was issued by the government, which mandated sesame and white pea beans to be traded only on the ECX. After having coffee mandated in 2008, we now have sesame and white pea beans also mandated to the ECX. Partly because of our prior work with the stakeholders and partly because of the experience coffee exporters had, the introduction of sesame and white pea beans in the exchange was comparatively smooth.

During the introduction of sesame and white pea beans, we worked a lot on developing stakeholder confidence and kept the stakeholders informed about everything that we were doing. Multiple forums were held at the sesame-producing areas in and around the Gondar region. This region was the stronghold of the deputy prime minister, and because of his support for the exchange, the sesame traders and the farmers were also quite positive about the ECX. Also, the ECX did not leave any stone unturned to reach out to the stakeholders. Dr. Eleni made numerous trips to Gondar to engage with stakeholders on a regular basis. Along with Dr. Eleni, Ben and Ahadu also made multiple trips to these areas and developed a very strong communication channel with the stakeholders.

This was something that helped us a lot. I remember one of the sessions where I was also asked to join as I was leading the development of the contract specifications.

I, along with Ben and Dr. Eleni, travelled to one of the sesame-producing areas, and we were driven to the meeting by our driver. As the meeting started, I could see a lot of people attending, and many of them were actually carrying guns with them. In that part of Ethiopia, carrying guns is part of the culture, and it is not something very unusual. The discussion started about sesame, and all the discussion was in Amharic, meaning I was not able to gather what it was pertaining to. However, what I could see was that there were people who were really angry, and my coffee experience told me that there was something very wrong. Ben and Dr. Eleni were listening to them very carefully, and I could not disturb them to help me understand what the discussion was about. As this was going on, I saw our project driver ready with the car just outside the gate of the meeting hall. I was sure that something serious was going on. Eventually I looked at Ben and asked him what the problem was. All that was happening was not sounding good to me, and I asked Ben, "What is the matter? Why are they so agitated?" Ben smiled at me and said, You know, there are a number of problems in this sesame sector, and they are explaining to us what problems we should solve. This made me a bit comfortable that they were not complaining or fighting with us but were trying to convince us to offer a solution that addressed their problems. But until Ben explains it to me, I know how scared I am and am not sure where it all is heading!

The introduction of sesame went very smoothly, and the exchange started trading in sesame and white pea beans by 2010. This helped us to significantly improve the trade values and the revenues at the exchange, and eventually, by January 2011, the exchange had achieved phenomenal success by recording US$1 billion worth of transactions executed on the exchange platform. The volume of the exchange in the financial year 2010–2011, courtesy of the stabilized market of coffee, sesame, and white pea beans, led the exchange to the Billion Dollar Club. This was a huge thing. I remember on February 11, 2011, the thousand days of the ECX were celebrated, and Dr. Eleni announced that the exchange had been able to trade commodities worth more than a billion dollars. As I attended that session, I was thinking about the period from 2008, when we planned to introduce coffee, and the journey till today, when we completed a thousand days of trading.

During this time, a lot of changes and experiences were recorded. It was an incredible feeling to be in that situation. Finally, we were winning and proving that the exchange market is the right solution for problems in Ethiopia. By the time sesame trading started at the exchange, in order to prove the exchange's worth, Dr. Eleni and I discussed how we could prove that the exchange had added value. I suggested that we conduct research about the percentage that the farmers earned out of the export value before and after the exchange started trading in sesame. I conducted that research, and it was proven that before the exchange started, the percentage of export value that farmers would get was little more than 30%, whereas after the exchange started trading, this had gone up to around 76%, which meant that farmers were getting a much higher percentage of the export value after the exchange started. When we dug deep into this, we realized that it was because a lot of the work that the exporters would do was not required now, and as a result, the exporters were making a lot of savings on their costs related to those services. This saving was ready to be transferred to the farmer, and because of this, the farmer was getting a higher percentage.

In fact, we were incentivizing the farmer to take better care of his product, and now that was leading to an overall improvement in the quality of the products, resulting in lower rejections. This was the success that we were looking for, and eventually my paper proved that. With this success, which we had achieved in sesame, white pea beans, and coffee, which were the important crops, we felt that the exchange should also go back to grains. The right opportunity came to us when the negotiations with the World Food Program began. The discussion materialized, and the World Food Program agreed to buy huge quantities for their supplies from the ECX in 2010. This was not easy, as this decision was taken after a lot of negotiation with the World Food Program. The World Food Program approved a policy of buying from the exchange rather than the conventional policy of tendering it. They realized that the policy of buying from the exchange would be transparent and would be the best replacement for the tendering process. As a result, the World Food Program started buying maize from the exchange platform, and close to five thousand plus tons of maize were procured by them. This was an important achievement for all of us, as now we could say that the exchange is not only trading in export commodities but also in grains. However, the disappointment was that the initial push by the World Food Program into maze trading. it could not be sustained, and as the World Food Program procurement slowed down, the grain trade also slowed down on the exchange.

All in all, from 2008, when we started, to 2011, significant achievements were recorded by the exchange. It had moved from a food security institution to a commercial trading platform offering unparalleled opportunities in the Ethiopian commodity export market. As the strategic plan of the ECX suggested, the exchange also increased its membership, and one hundred and fifty new membership seats were auctioned for the membership. When the exchange had started, the membership was offered at a starting price of the birr equivalent of five thousand dollars, which was now offered on a competitive bidding system. People bid for the seat, and eventually the highest bidder got the seat. A huge response was received for the seat allocation auction, and the highest bid was in excess of three hundred thousand dollars, which was a phenomenal achievement for an exchange like the ECX.

By 2011, the exchange had started trading an average of six million dollars every day, which was supported by 100% physical deliveries, meaning that products or commodities worth six million dollars per day were being exchanged. This was, by no means, an ordinary achievement, and this made the ECX a benchmark of success, not only in Ethiopia but overall in Africa and also in the developing world. Many publications have recorded the phenomenal rise of the ECX and have praised the changes we brought to the Ethiopian commodity markets. The exchange's entry into the billion-dollar club was the result of the tireless efforts of multiple people. It was cohesive teamwork that resulted in the exchange achieving this success. Though most of the publications and media coverage circled around Dr. Eleni, as the architect and champion of the commodity exchange in Ethiopia, it was the team that delivered on critical occasions. It was not only building warehouse structures or an IT system; a lot of other things were also done to achieve this success. Right from the beginning, the ECX had a very focused strategy on market data. How would the price-related information of the exchange be spread out, and how would this be made available to the farmers? Elaborate projects were done on the market data with the financial support of the World Bank as part of the project funding to achieve this. Apart from the input, internal price display boards were installed on the trading floor and became the hallmark of the exchange floor. Multiple remote-access electronic display boards were set up throughout the rural locations in Ethiopia. More than 25 rural locations had these display boards, which were monitored from the central office in Addis Ababa.

There was a dedicated team led by Ahadu that was looking at these installations and the maintenance of the price display boards. The impact of the price display board was indirect, but in any manner no less than any other effort. These price display boards were critical to the rural population of Ethiopia, who would now get the information almost immediately. This eventually played a major role in building confidence about the exchange. A lot of work was about building the traders confidence in the exchange. It was important that the traders felt that the ECX was there to listen to their concerns and address them in a positive manner. This was something that Ben had mastered, and his effort in building relationships with the traders for the exchange was something that brought a lot of confidence between the exchange and its members.

The members could discuss their issues openly with the exchange, and the exchange would respond pragmatically to these issues. This relationship was the basis of the success that ECX was achieving. When the core functions of trading warehousing, clearing settlement, and IT kept bringing in innovations and changes, support services like market data and customer relationship management also played a major role. Above all, it was the trust and the efforts done in a coordinated and effective manner that were the hallmarks of the success of the ECX.

CHAPTER ELEVEN

LIFE AT THE ECX

When I came to join the ECX in February 2008, little did I know that the ECX was going to transform my whole professional life. It was by far the most encouraging and learning period of my life, both professionally and personally. Professionally, the exposure I got to the commodity exchange was unparalleled, and the opportunity to serve the United Nations was something I could not even dream of earlier. But it was the ECX that gave me both those opportunities. It was not only a learning experience but also a satisfying experience doing something that could add value to a country's economy. It had, in fact, led to a lot of changes in countries like Ethiopia. Being in Ethiopia was, professionally, a golden period of my career, and sometimes I still miss those golden days.

As you must have realized by now, the ECX was always a happening place. It was not a typical United Nations organization's job where, in the morning, you go to your desk, work, and by the evening, you are done. Not that the UN job is not an important job, but the routine nature is what I am referring to. We were more like a highly competitive private sector company or even a start-up, ensuring that our work stays ahead of the curve and that we are able to remain ahead in the market. The flexibility, resilience, and capacity to adapt that I developed while working with the ECX are things that I still count on, and a lot of credit goes to those days for making me what I am today. Close to four years with ECX were full of excitement and varied experiences. The ECX project was a component of multiple projects in a way, and each project was led by a competent person with his team.

When I first saw the trading floor, I was really impressed with the way it was designed. As I said, it was an octagonal floor with a viewer gallery, offices, and trading clerks sitting around the floor. The octagonal model, however, was the real feature of the trading floor. With the price display boards installed on the trading floor, the floor looked like a highly professional place. The first project that the exchange took up after the launch was the installation of price display boards. The World Bank had supported the ECX with a rural infrastructure development assistance fund, which was allocated to the Ministry of Agriculture and Rural Development. The Government decided to allocate it to the ECX for the installation of price display boards in the exchange as well as in rural areas across Ethiopia. This was a competitive bid and was won by a company called Wavetech from Dubai. The company was originally a Pakistani company but had moved its offices to Dubai. This is when I first met Zia. Zia was an exceptionally talented and very humble individual. He was representing Wavetech, and when we had a discussion with him, he came up with multiple ideas that made our strategy better and more useful.

Prior to this, the price display boards, which are LED display boards, were procured from a Chinese vendor. The initial boards were really small and not very impressive. The biggest challenge with these boards was that when any change in the display layout was to be made, it had to be done by the vendor's engineer. The Chinese engineer coming and doing it meant that every change in the display board would cost the exchange a significant amount of money. This was not a sustainable model, and we were looking for alternatives. It was then that Wavetech participated in the World Bank bid. As we started to work with them after they were successful in the bid, they offered some very innovative and interesting solutions. Back then, in 2009, the display board or LED display market was dominated by European companies, and Wavetech was one of the very few Asian companies that was emerging strong in the competition, making it difficult for the Europeans. We found Wavetech solutions to be very affordable and easy to manage. Besides, as we started working with them, the professionalism they showed was beyond expectations.

Once the boards that were installed on the trading floor were lit up and trading started, the whole environment of the trading floor significantly changed. The aesthetics of the trading floor became different, and nobody would believe that we were on a trading floor in Ethiopia. Also, the outdoor boards that they supplied were wonderful, as there was an in-built redundancy in the system on the boards that helped counter the network connectivity issue. The boards could be connected via

SMS also and updated based on that information, which meant that they were no longer dependend to be on the internet, which was a big relief. During those days in Ethiopia, internet spread was not so great, and the down times were very high, making the relevance and effectiveness of the board come under question. But the solution offered by Wavetech made things much easier. Also, what Wavetech offered was a template-based price display configuration, which meant that the technical person at the market data department could make changes in the display design of the board using the display software, and we could display whatever data we wanted to, based on the design template. The changes in the template design could be done internally. These were some significant changes that were brought in due to the display boards supplied by Wavetech. The market data department was led by Ahadu Woubshet, who had very strong experience in this sector. He not only contributed to bringing one of the best boards for display but also led the project to develop a SMS IVR system, which later connected thousands of farmers in Ethiopia to the Exchange. Daily, hundreds of telephone calls were handled by these SMS and IVR systems. These systems definitely made a significant change in the perception of Ethiopia's commodity exchange.

My professional life in Ethiopia's commodity exchange was exciting and challenging at the same time. In the initial days, when the coffee was started, I would be sitting down next to the trading floor and observing each and every moment to ensure that nothing went wrong and that whatever happened on the floor, I was in total control of it. I was supported by a wonderful team of staff, which included Abenet Bekele, who was the manager and one of the strongest pillars in the department. We also had a floor supervisor, Fekadu, who was very effective in his job and played his role with a lot of honesty and commitment. He initially came in as a floor representative of EGTE during the initial days of trading, but soon realized that the exchange may offer him a better career prospect and joined the exchange. I was especially thrilled to have him on the team.

Apart from these two, we had an assistant manager for trade reconciliations who would look at the trades and ensure that all the correct trades were properly recorded. Initially, this role was played by a gentleman called Daniel Yilkal, but soon Daniel was moved to the clearing and settlement department, and we got a replacement in the form of another gentleman, Samson Gebremichel. Samson was also very effective and very minute in his observations. He would observe the tickets very minutely and ensure that no data entry error ever happened. It was a notable fact that, in spite of hundreds of transactions happening daily, not a single transaction was wrongly recorded or registered. Going by that fact, the margin for error was probably less than 0.001 percent, which was a significant achievement for the department and its wonderful team. The traders on the floor would fill out the trading tickets and give them to the trade entry clerks.

We had a team of six trade entry clerks who would do the data entry into the system for recording the trade. Because people were under pressure for trade, they would very quickly fill out the tickets and hand them over to the trade entry clerk, who had to be equally quick in reading and posting the right details into the system. This thing then went to Samson, who would ensure that the data entry was properly done and that no error in any form of trade was registered. Once he was done, he would close the session and move on to the next session. We had sequential sessions, and the morning was reserved for the grains and the afternoon for coffee. The coffee trade would start at 2 p.m. (European time) and continue until 5:30 or 6 p.m. . Sometimes, depending on the season and the supplies, it would be even later. When the sesame and white pea beans came, they occupied the morning slot.

When we started with coffee, all of us were anxious and very focused on ensuring that no error happened, as the volumes were significantly jumping to higher levels and we were not sure if our systems and people would be able to correctly respond to these increased volumes and increased pressure. It was not only the volume but also the time pressure, as these sessions had to be completed within the given time and moved to the next section. Any delay in organizing this session or closing this session would mean that the next session would be delayed, and this would be a disaster for the time management at the exchange.

Given this, everybody of us was particular about ensuring that these sessions went smoothly and no delays happened. On one of the initial days, I remember we had to start this session by 2 p.m., and I had instructed my team to be ready by 1:30 p.m. so that there was no surprise at the time of starting the session. However, when I reached the floor at 1.25 p.m., I could not find the session open in the trading system. I inquired with

Abenet about why the trading system is not on and why we have not started with the details to be filled in. I was told that because the IT team wanted to ensure that sessions happened in their presence, they had not opened the session. I was really upset as, because of this delay, we might actually cause a delay in the start of the trading session. But then I saw, at 1:30 p.m. , the technology manager, Tedla, walk into the trading floor. I was a bit upset and told him that he should be here before 1:30 p.m. . He was surprised and said to me, "But 12:30 p.m. to 1:30 p.m. is national lunch time. This is the time that everybody takes their lunch. So how can I come before 1:30 p.m.?" I was not amused by the answer at the time, but when I look back today, I think it was an interesting one. Tedla, for that matter, was one of the most qualified technical experts we had in the IT department, and he should be credited with developing the system in a very short span of time. Of course, he had the support and guidance of Solomon, who brought a lot of ideas into the trading system, but executing those ideas and making them happen was Tedla's job.

Tedla was very well supported by other team members like Elias and Iyobe. In the initial days, Ribka Makonnen and Mickias were also there in the department; they were from a very early stage of the system's development. These people did a wonderful job ensuring that the system does not have downtime and towards responding to all the changes that were required in a very short span of time. It was nothing short of a miracle that in less than four months, a new version of the trading system was rolled out that would accommodate coffee and was able to stand the stress test in a live environment as the coffee season started to pick up. This system continued for a pretty long period of time before the ECX moved into the electronic system.

The adaptation of electronic systems is also, in itself, an interesting story. Initially, it was thought that the MCX system would be procured, but due to multiple reasons, the MCX system could not be prepared, and we had moved to a floor-based trading system. However, going forward, by 2009–2010, we realized that now the time has come to get into an electronic trading platform, which would itself take about eight months to a year to get operational. The World Bank, under the same rural infrastructure development project, had identified a budget for the technology procurement by the ECX as well. The project was led by Solomon, and we all contributed to developing the specifications for the system that would be used to procure it. The first procurement was initiated in 2009, when only two companies responded to the tender that the Exchange had floated. These two companies were Securities Trading Technologies from South Africa, which had supplied its technology for the SAFEX market in Johannesburg, and Millennium IT, which was, during that time, emerging and had supplied technology to some developing markets.

However, on the evaluation of the bids, we realized that none of the bidders qualified or offered the solutions that we were looking at, and the procurement from any one of these two bidders would mean that we were not able to match our business model with the software that they were providing. Hence, we informed the World Bank that the technology vendors were not able to provide what we were looking for, and as a result, the tender was cancelled. Again in 2010, the tender was floated, and this time more companies applied for the tender. Even Financial Technology, which was the parent company of MCX, was also in the play. The tender was evaluated by a team set up by Dr. Eleni, which included myself, Dr. Kadri, Solomon, Ahadu, and our CFO, Yonas. We looked at the tenders submitted by each of the parties and had a very detailed discussion on each submission.

Again, this time we realized that none of the bidders could match up to the technical requirements that we had specified, and hence we had to cancel the tender. During this, some oversights happened by Solomon, which I believe were genuine oversights. I don't want to go into the details of these oversights, but I have to add that these oversights could have been avoided. In one of the oversights, the bid amount posted on the World Bank website for one of the tender participants was increased by ten times. It was an error in typing, as a zero had also been added while typing. Technically, it was a typo error but had a damaging impact. Immediately, a letter was sent to the ECX and the World Bank, claiming that there was malpractice and that this should be looked into. We realized our mistake, and immediately the information was pulled down and revised information was posted. The typo error was corrected; however, it did not stop there, and a lot of complaints were made. Eventually, the World Bank looked at it, and no merit in the case was found. The World Bank believed that these were genuine errors and did not call for a detailed inquiry.

However, because of this, we were not able to utilize the funds provided by the World Bank in the given span of time. As per the World Bank regulations, the fund that the bank allocates has to be utilized before a deadline, and because we could not find a suitable vendor, the technology was not procured. This meant that the fund reserved for the technology was withdrawn by the World Bank because of the expiration of the time limit. This did not go well with the government, and the prime minister's office ordered an investigation into the whole matter. This investigation was to see if there was a deliberate reason not to select the bidders or if there was any malpractice in the process. Unfortunately, when this investigation started, the prime responsibility was pushed with Solomon, and he ended up having to fight this battle on his own.

All of us in the committee were called to the prime minister's office, and a discussion happened. Eventually, Solomon provided all the documents and details to the prime minister's office, which got convinced that there was no malpractice and the complaints made were not substantiated, which was a big relief. The matter was closed, and the relief was that our integrity was not questioned. However, what that meant was that the ECX lost an opportunity to procure a world-class technology platform for its trading system. Later, in the coming years, Solomon built a system that the ECX uses. Subsequently, as Solomon started his IT company, this system was also bought by the Ghana Commodity Exchange from Solomon's company. After this, the matter subsided, and it was never talked about again. In this case, all of us felt that Dr. Eleni, being the leader of the organization, should have fought this battle and not left Solomon to do the justifications. She was equally involved in all the decision-making processes and was regularly updated about what was happening. As a result, she could have taken on the role of leader and defended the exchange against the case in the prime minister's office. But for some reasons best known to her, she chose not to do so, and the team had to do it on their own.

It was not the first time that Dr. Eleni lost the confidence of the team. In September 2010, the Ethiopian birr was devalued by the National Bank of Ethiopia. This devaluation was a significant one, and this meant that all the prices of the export commodities were to be readjusted. The market was put into a tizzy, and we had to take a decision on opening the price limits so that the prices could readjust and we could re-install the price limits after the re-adjustment. The day this decision happened, Dr. Eleni was in Ghana, making some presentations, and the responsibility of acting CEO for the first time was left on Dr. Kadri Alfah. Dr. Kadri was authorized to attend to regular matters and was not given the powers to take critical decisions like this. As the session timing approached, we were looking to open the session for trade, but the traders refused to trade unless and until the price circuits were opened and the market was allowed to re-adjust. This decision, as per the rules, was within the decision-making powers of the CEO, who was out of the country. We were stuck on what to do. Somehow, Dr. Eleni was contacted, and she agreed to a proposal to open the price circuit limits that day for the prices to re-adjust. A lot of people felt that Dr. Eleni knew this devaluation was going to come and did not brief the team beforehand. I am not sure if she knew it, but this was a time when the team was divided on the opinion.

ECX, in spite of all its challenges, was able to create a global benchmark, and a lot of people visited the ECX from 2009 onwards. I particularly remember one day walking into the office and being told that a guest had come and that I, Ben, and Ahahdu should meet him. Dr. Eleni was not in office that day, and we were asked to represent the Exchange's management in the meeting. I was not sure who the guest was, and as I walked into the meeting, I asked the lady who had informed me about this meeting who the guest was, and she very coolly said, "It's Howard Buffett." In the next 5 minutes, I was sitting in front of Howard Buffett, son of Warren Buffett, the world's number one stock Trader. This was an exciting meeting where Howard, who was on an Africa tour, wanted to meet the exchange and see how it has been working. We explained to him everything that we do, and the interest with which he was listening to it was really exciting. We could see that he was really amazed to see that in a country like Ethiopia, which does not seem to have those capital market structures, such a professional institution is working and working fine. The structures that we explained to him were of international standards, and he was really appreciative of that. This was a meeting that I remembered for a long period of time.

However, it was not only Howard who visited the ECX; many other celebrities also visited the exchange. These celebrities include Helena Clark, the then Secretary General for UNDP. UNDP was one of the financing institutions for the ECX and was providing technical assistance to the ECX. This was a success story that UNDP took a lot of pride in talking about. This was the reason that when Helena Clark visited Ethiopia, this was an institution that she would visit. She came to the trading floor to ring the bell, as is customary at the ECX. Whenever any high-ranking dignitary would visit, we would invite him to ring the bell and start the market. Helena Clark also rang the bell on the day of her visit to the ECX.

Apart from Helena Clark, another visitor that ECX received was Melinda Gates. In 2009, when Bill and Melinda Gates were visiting Ethiopia, Melinda Gates visited the ECX. During the visit, Melinda Gates spent around one hour understanding the whole exchange operations and the impact of the exchange operations on the Ethiopian economy. Like any other foreign dignitary, Melinda Gates was highly surprised by the sophistication that the exchange was bringing in and the ease with which people had adjusted to this sophistication. Melinda also interacted with all the team members and appreciated our efforts to bring this market to Ethiopia.

ECX also received the then-president of the World Bank, Robert Zollick, in the first week of 2010. Robert Zollick was on an Africa tour, and Ethiopia was a destination for him. He had come to Ethiopia to meet with various African leaders who had gathered at the African Union, during his three-day visit. He visited the ECX and understood how the exchange is bringing about a change in coffee trading in Ethiopia. This was again a proud project that the World Bank would showcase to different stakeholders around the world as the Exchange had become a big success. Robert Zollick spent a lot of time sitting in the meeting room, asking individually how the exchange operations are run and how they are making changes to the Ethiopian economy. As with all the past visitors, he too was very impressed with the way the exchange was put together.

The real success of the exchange, which the traders could feel on a daily basis, was the smooth trading sessions. The trading session could be so smooth because of the very strong teamwork within the trading department. I had a very strong team. This team would work very closely with me, and to a certain extent, Abenet and I developed such a close working relationship that he would understand what I would need and what my instructions would be. He would prepare for it well in advance and make my work very easy. I particularly remember one gesture that the trading department made, which I will never forget in my life. In May 2010, I was awarded my PhD after successfully defending my thesis in India. By the end of May, I will return to Ethiopia with a PhD degree. By 2010, systems had stabilized, and I would not go to the trading floor before the start. The team was handling it wonderfully.

That day, Abenet came to me and told me that today I should come and ring the bell. I didn't suspect anything and went and rang the bell. When I rang the bell, the announcement was made by the floor supervisor, Fekadu, in Amharic, that our boss is here and he has now completed his PhD and should be referred to as Dr. Bharat. Everybody started clapping, and I was overwhelmed! They also organized a cake for me to cut to celebrate the success of my PhD. This was a gesture that I will never forget in my life.

By 2011, my work was also getting noticed outside Ethiopia, and as part of the ECX senior management team, I got the opportunity to meet a lot of people. One of the high points in my career came when I was invited to speak at the UNCTAD Global Commodity Forum about the commodity exchanges in Ethiopia. It was a particularly respectable invitation, and I felt proud to be at the UNCTAD, speaking on the Global Commodities Forum. Little did I know that it was just the beginning, and for the next five to six years, I continued to speak at the global commodities forum every year on their invitation. I travelled to Geneva on January 30th, 2011 and attended the forum in Geneva. This was my first trip to Europe, and I made a lot of memories that I cherished. I was introduced, through a common friend, to the Chief of Staff of the Secretary General's office at that time. He was an Ethiopian, a wonderful person called Tesfachew. Tesfachew also introduced me to Dr. Supachi, the Secretary-General of UNCTAD. This started my relationship with UNCTAD, and I got several invitations to speak at various forums organized by UNCTAD.

In March 2011, I was also invited by the Confederation of Indian Industries to speak at the CII-EXIM Bank India Africa project partnership summit, which was organized in Delhi. This was particularly important because it was setting the tone for the upcoming India-Africa Forum Summit, which was to be held in Addis Ababa in May 2011.

Back in Addis, in February 2011, the ECX had also organized a conference, where multiple African commodity exchanges represented and participated. One of the guests that I met and was particularly happy to meet was Dr. Ramsheshan, the then managing director of NCDEX India. Dr. Ramseshan is a wonderful gentleman to meet, and being an Indian, we discussed a lot of details about how the spot market in Ethiopia has been built. That was the time when Mr. Ramaseshan was looking to build a spot market at NCDEX as well and was particularly interested in our experiences.

Overall, the professional life in the ECX was challenging and also rewarding. It gave me a lot of satisfaction when we saw the way people were benefiting. In the year 2009, after one year of coffee trading, there was a get-together organized by the group of akrabis, who were very thankful to the ECX for bringing coffee into the exchange system. Their support throughout the coffee crisis, if I can call it that, gave us a lot of strength and a lot of belief that this crisis would be over. On the one hand, the exporters were agitated and opposed the exchange, and on the other hand, the akrabis were standing tall in support of the exchange and saying that this is the right decision that the government has taken. After one year of coffee trading, they invited the whole management team for a get-together, where we were praised and thanked for giving them the opportunity to be on an equal footing with the exporters in the market. That gesture of the akrabis was really heart-warming and very motivating.

When I look back at the efforts that I had put in to make coffee trade on the ECX, I realize that a lot of Innovations were brought into the ECX, and I had a lot to learn professionally from all my team members and colleagues. A lot of that knowledge that I gained is still useful to me, and I will always be thankful to be an ECX team member.

CHAPTER TWELVE

The Socialites in Addis

When I moved to Addis Ababa in February 2008, I decided to go alone, as I was not sure how much time I would spend in Addis. I was not sure, after five months of my initial contract, what the status would be. I did not want to disturb my family and decided to go alone. It was a time when I had to explore new things and set up everything before it was comfortable for my family to move in. My daughter at the time was about 2 years old and just starting school. By then, I had not decided to settle down in Addis Ababa for the long term.

When I moved to Addis in the initial days, the work pressure was so great that I did not get any chance to socialize and get to know people. One day, while returning from the office, I saw an Indian couple just below my apartment. I smiled at them, and they returned the smile and started talking to me. They were very courteous and interesting people to talk to. They asked me where I worked, to which I told them I worked for the ECX Project. They did not know the project, and I explained to them that it was a contract with IFPRI, which they recognized. In the conversation, I learned that they worked for Addis Ababa University. At that time, under the UNDP support program, a lot of Indian teachers were recruited and were working with different universities in Ethiopia. Most of them were working with Addis Ababa University. As I have said previously, Indians have a strong history in the education sector in Ethiopia, and right from school to university, a lot of Indian teachers have been employed. Under the UNDP assistance program, funding assistance is given to the Ethiopian government to recruit Indian teachers at competitive salaries. The UNDP paid a certain sum of money to the Ethiopian government for this. This assistance enabled the Ethiopian government to hire a lot of Indian teachers.

The couple I met introduced themselves as Dr. Vishnu Sharma and Dr. Sanchita Sharma. In the conversation, I learned that they also stayed on the same floor of the apartment as I did. I was in one corner of the building, and they were in the other corner of the building. The building was divided into two blocks, with each block having a door. That's why I did not know about them. I was happy that there is an Indian family that stays in the building that I can reach out to for any help. They were very helpful, and we started meeting quite often. I was alone, and this was my first social acquaintance with the Indian people in Addis. The Sharma couple worked as professors at the Veterinary College in Addis Ababa, and their children, a son and a daughter, studied at the Indian National School. The Indian National School was for the Indian community in Ethiopia. At one point in time, it used to be the most popular school in Addis. The school was a community school, and the Hindu Mahajan community of Addis was running the Indian National School. The school was located in the piazza area of the old town of Addis Ababa.

The Sharma couple were originally from Jaipur and were in Addis Ababa under the UNDP assistance program. Dr. Sharma told me that the building we were staying in was actually meant for subsidized housing and was rented by the government to various Ethiopian nationals. A lot of these apartments were given to the university to accommodate their professors, and the university had allocated these houses to the Indian professors that were staying in Ethiopia. Dr. Sharma was very particular about the location of our apartment, and he considered it to be the best location in Addis Ababa to stay. He was right, as it was a very well connected place and everything, from groceries to restaurants, was very close. We developed very good relations until they moved back to India in September 2008.

When my family joined in May 2008, they were the first people we interacted with. They invited us to their place, and we also did. We were settling down in Addis, and we did not have a lot of opportunities to invite guests at that time. My wife, Runa was finding it difficult to adjust to life in Addis Ababa. Multiple challenges we were facing. Though Dr. Sharma and his wife tried to help us with everything possible, settling down was not that easy. The first challenge that we realized after my family joined was that the house we were staying in was not facing the road, like Dr. Sharma's house, which meant that when you looked out of the window, you would see only other houses and no people. Even within the building, we would not see anyone. Since my daughter, Urvi, was very young, taking her down and upstairs in the apartment building used to be a challenge. As a result, for several weeks initially, Runa found it very difficult to cope with the feeling of isolation. She felt totally cut off from the people, which made it difficult to adjust. It was so much so that we did not unpack what we brought for two months, not sure if Runa and Urvi would continue staying in Addis or not.

The second challenge we encountered was with grocery supplies. More specifically, with milk. The availability of packed milk was also difficult during those times in Addis. We would go to the supermarket to be told that the milk stock was finished. As the supply was very short, the supermarket would not give more than one pack of milk to one customer. Urvi was small, and we needed more milk. For this, we had to look at different supermarkets to get the milk. Later, Runa was able to convince one of the supermarkets to give her one extra pack daily. It was not a very easy situation for other groceries, either. We tried to find out where we could get Indian supplies and vegetables. Basic Indian groceries like spices, dall, and vegetables were difficult to find in the supermarkets in Addis, as they were not like Kenya or Tanzania, where Indian vegetables and supplies would be available more widely.

There were very few shops that would sell Indian supplies, specifically dall, Atta, and vegetables. Dr. Sharma told us to go to "Japan market,", where every Indian family goes to shop, and we can get everything basic that we need in our grocery supplies. Mrs. Sharma also offered that she would ask her maid to come with us so we could find it easily. On a Saturday morning, we dressed up and went to the "Japan market". As we got down from the taxi, we realized that Japan market is not a modern market; it was a very local market with a lot of mud and dirt! It was only called Japan market because the location was behind the Japanese embassy in Addis Ababa. People looked at us as we were well dressed up and were confused about why somebody would dress up so much to come to a market like this.

Only an Indian in Addis would realize how important the Japan market was, and for all the time we stayed in Addis, it used to be the market for groceries for us. The good thing was that everything that we required we would get there except the ground spices and the Toor dall, which we had to carry from India. The initial days were very difficult for Runa to adjust to the new environment. Though Mrs. Sharma helped us find a very good maid, but the problem was that she would not understand English, and Runa would not understand Amharic. This meant that they had to communicate only in sign language! It used to be difficult, as explaining the maid in sign language was a challenge in itself. Except for me, Urvi, and occasionally the Sharma family, Runa did not have anybody to speak to. Still, Runa and I were somehow trying to settle down.

Ethiopia had an acute power shortage at that time, and once a week, the power would be off in the evening for three to four hours. Normally, the power would go out at six p.m. and return only at nine p.m. This was before Ethiopia became self-sufficient in electricity, and power shortages were common. It would be very depressing in the house, with no power and no light from outside to come in. To avoid that, we would go to a restaurant and sit there waiting for power to come back. The restaurant was a few blocks away and was an open-air restaurant on the 7th floor. We could sit down on the terrace and see if the power has returned to our apartment. Once we see that, we will walk back to our apartment. At that time, Urvi was just about two years old, and for her to walk seven floors up was not possible. I used to carry her while climbing the stairs. It used to be difficult, but I enjoyed it.

In one of the discussions, Dr. Sharma mentioned the Indian National School. Initially, we went to the school to seek admission for Urvi. In the course of discussion, the Principle, Murli Nair, asked Runa if she was interested in joining. Runa had just completed her E.C.C.Ed course from India and was keen to explore opportunities as a teacher. This was a perfect opportunity. Though we did not put Urvi in the Indian National School, Runa decided to apply there as a teacher. Following the application, she was invited for the interview, and finally she was selected. From the next academic year, which would start in September, she was to join the Indian National School as a teacher. This was a big relief, as now she would start a job, ensuring that she would be able to settle down much more easily. This was early July, and by then I had also gotten the offer letter from the United Nations Development Program. Now, we were getting settled in Addis slowly.

Before Runa and Urvi joined me in Addis, they had to get their passports. For them to apply for a passport, I was required to send a notarized document for the passport's issuance. I went to the Indian embassy in Addis to get the document issued. The Indian embassy took all the documents from me and told me to come in the evening to collect the notarized certificate. As I went in the evening, I was a bit early and was waiting for the document delivery at the embassy. I met another gentleman like me, waiting for a similar document. I started speaking to him, and he introduced himself as Jayant Jakhde, and was working for Bajaj Motorcycles. In Ethiopia, Bajaj was selling motorcycles, and now it was setting up an assembly plant. He was looking after the finances and the factory operations. He was from Pune, and being a Maharashtrian, I immediately connected with him. We exchanged our contact details and remained in touch until our families joined in. After a family reunion, my daughter and his daughter were in the same school. Runa and his wife developed a good friendship, which also helped Runa settle down in Addis. Jayant, his wife, and his colleague Umesh and his wife were the guests we had on Urvi's birthday in 2008.

I was in office in February 2008 one day, and the membership drive is going on. Ben introduced me to an Indian man named Mahendra Patel, who had come to understand the membership requirements of the ECX. I was interested to meet Mahendra Bhai and realized he was a very humble and nice individual. We immediately connected, and he introduced me to his colleague, Govind. We exchanged numbers, and Mahendra bhai told me to reach out to him if I needed any help. One day, while I was climbing up the stairs at the apartment building, I met Govind and asked him how come he was there. He told me that he has some friends from Uganda who are planning to set up a business in Ethiopia, and he was there to meet them. He introduced me to another Indian family that was planning a relocation from Addis Ababa. The people I met were Shyam Agarwal and his brother-in-law, Vikash. It was just that formal introduction that remained for a few months before we connected.

Mahendra Bhai also introduced me to the Director of his company. Mahendra Bhai was working for a company called Export Trading Group (ETG), which is a large conglomerate originating out of Tanzania and has a very strong presence throughout Africa. The company was owned by an Indian Tanzanian, Mahesh Bhai Patel, and Pradeep Bhai was his younger brother. When Pradeep Bhai visited Addis, Mahendra Bhai introduced me to him. Pradeep Bhai invited me for lunch, and we had a formal introduction. Since then, Pradeep Bhai and I have kept in touch, and whenever Pradeep Bhai would be in Addis, he would call me and we would meet. In spite of being the director of one of the biggest conglomerates in East Africa, Pradeep Bhai was very down-to-earth and humble in his nature. He was based in Kenya, and when I went to Kenya in 2009, Pradeep Bhai hosted me in Nairobi. Unfortunately, Pradeep Bhai passed away a few years ago, but until his death, we kept a very strong connection.

Mahendra Bhai was also helpful when we were looking for the school for Urvi. We had gone to the Indian

National School, but did not want to put her there. Mahendra Bhai suggested about the Greek Community School, which was much better, and a lot of Indian kids used to study there. The Greek Community School also had a lot of Indian teachers, and that made us more comfortable. I tried to secure admission at the Greek Community School for Urvi, which she got. After the initial two to three months, we felt that this is somewhere that we can settle down at least for a few years, I remember Dr. Sharma used to say “Initially, you would feel that this is not the right place for you and you cannot live here. But I am telling you that on the day you have to leave, you would feel that we don’t want to leave this place". Runa said to me, "How can this happen? How can somebody settle down in a country like this so much that he does not want to leave? I don’t think that is going to happen to us." That was exactly the same feeling on our last day in Addis, and we remembered Dr. Sharma for his words.

By now we had started to explore more about the Indian community and the city of Addis and started to be socially active. With the jobs in our hands and Urvi’s admission confirmed, e and Runa realized that we would continue to stay in Addis. We started to like the place as we started to make some social connections, mainly through Mahendra Bhai. Mahendra Bhai introduced Mahendra Bhai to the Hindu Mahajan community in Addis, which was socially active and would organize several events where people could participate and interact with the Indian community. The first event at which we participated was a movie show. We really missed movies in Addis, as theatres did not play Indian movies. Though the Indian movies were very popular, they were more popular on DVDs and CDs than in theatres. The Hindu Mahajan community organized a show of a recently released movie at the Indian National School. Mahendra Bhai told me about that, and we were very happy to buy the tickets. He helped us buy the tickets, and we showed up at the movie show. Mahindra bhai introduced us to a lot of people, and during that time we got introduced to the same people who had interviewed Runa for the job at the Indian National School. Some people with whom we had a very strong bond while in Addis, and we got introduced to them that day, were Mayur Bhai Kothari and Bhavin Bhai Shah. I found them to be very friendly and helpful towards the Indian community.

While coming back from the movie show, we were struggling to get a taxi, and Mahendra Bhai helped us by introducing us to Sanjay Purohit. Mr. Sanjay Purohit was Mahendra Bhai's friend and was working with a plastic tank manufacturing company in Addis Ababa. Since he was staying in the same area as us, he offered to drop us off at our apartment. When he reached our apartment, he asked me if I knew Shyam Agrawal. I told him that I had met him. Sanjay Purohit told me that he is a good friend. That was my first interaction with Sanjay bhai, and as we spent more time in Addis, Sanjay's family and my family group became very close. Sanjay bhai and his wife Sandhya bhabhi, their son Rahul, and their very young daughter Jhanvi all became very close to us. Later next year, Sanjay's younger brother Sachin and his wife Alka also joined, and we used to have weekly get-togethers and spend a lot of time with each other. It took time for us to develop that strong bond with Sanjay bhai, but it was

Mahendra who introduced me to a lot of Indians in Addis and helped me settle down with the social life in Addis.

Once I was walking up the stairs at the apartment I stayed, I met Vikash downstairs. Vikash and I started chatting, and he told me that every Sunday he, Shyam bhai, Sanjay bhai, and many other people go to the Indian Embassy to play cricket. He asked me if I would like to join. I was very keen and told him that I would love to However, in a few days, both Vikash and I had a shock to bear. In the early weeks of October, I tried to reach out to Viskash and Shyam Bhai. I knocked on the door of their apartment, and an Ethiopian lady opened it. I asked about them, and she refused, saying that nobody by that name stays here. I was confused because just two days ago, I had met Vikash, and he did not say anything about moving out of that apartment. Then I met Sanjay bhai and asked him if he knew what happened. By then I had started to communicate with Sanjay bhai more regularly, and when I asked him what happened, he told me that the landlord had asked them to vacate the apartment in two days, and they were in very deep trouble. They had to find an alternate house and relocate in two days. I felt shocked, and I told Runa about this. I said, "How can a landlord ask you to vacate in two days? This is really very bad."

The next day, my landlord also called and then came to meet me. During the meeting, he told me that he would like me to vacate the house, and it has to be done immediately. Though he did not give us only two days, he gave us about a month to vacate. We had already paid rent for the house for three months, and one month of that was remaining. He told us that we can stay for this month, and after that, we will have to move. There was probably a crackdown by the government, where they were trying to find people subletting the subsidized apartments. We started searching the house and realized that it was very difficult. We had our specifications for the house. Most of the houses in Addis Ababa are villas. These villas were built as a main villa and a small quarter behind it. The main villa was rented to an expat, and the back unit would be used by the owners to stay. For our privacy and based on the United Nations Security parameters, we wanted a villa that was independent. We were also specific about the location, and the price that we were ready to pay with all these constraints made it difficult to find a house. It was mandatory for any UN employee to get the clearance from the Staff Security Department before occupying the house.

We were introduced to a real estate agent called Mr. Tito. Mr. Tito was a wonderful gentleman and worked very hard to find a suitable house for us. Finally, he found a house where the same two-unit structures were there. But the front unit was a villa with two bedrooms, and the back unit was a smaller unit with one bedroom and one small room, along with a lounge and kitchen. The front villa was occupied by an Indian working on rural electrification projects for a company called KEC International. He was courteous enough to tell the owners that if they want to rent out the front villa to us, they can do so, and he would shift to the back villa as he was staying alone. We liked the front villa and agreed to rent it. We thought that it would be good socially. The person staying in that house was Mr. Ram Krishnan, who is an engineer from Karnataka. Just before Diwali 2008, we moved to this house, which was our home until we left it in 2011.

Our landlady, Sisay, was a wonderful lady, and we had a very cordial relationship with her. She would help us with anything we needed. Her nature made us stay in that house throughout our stay in Addis. We moved to our new house in Bole, Rwanda, just a day before Diwali 2008. We were trying to figure out what celebrations are held on Diwali. We came to know that Hindu Mahajan has celebrations, and we purchased the passes for those events. We attended all the functions of Hindu Mahajan, and by then, because of Runa's teaching at the Indian National School, we had a much bigger social circle. This was our first social interaction in many months.

The Indian Embassy also organizes a function every year on Diwali. This year also, it was planned, and we planned to attend. When we were in our apartment, Mrs. Sharma introduced Runa to Nishi Sharma, the wife of Naveen Sharma, who worked at the Indian Embassy. Runa came to know that the Indian Embassy was going to organize celebration for Diwali festival where a fashion show featuring Indian traditional dresses was to be organized. Naveen and Nishi Sharma's daughter was interested in wearing the traditional Marathi nauari saree, but not knowing how.

Mrs. Sanchita Sharma asked my wife if she could help, and Runa readily agreed. Mr. Sharma told Nishi Ji and her daughter to come to our place so that the discussion could happen. That was our first interaction with Naveen Ji and Nishi Ji. As Nishi ji visited with her daughter Nikita, Runa was also introduced to Mrs. Upma Ranjan, whose husband, Dr. Rajesh Ranjan, was the first secretary at the Indian Embassy that time. The next time we met Naveen ji and his family was when Dr. Vishnu Sharma was leaving Addis. Due to some reason, the Diwali function at the Indian embassy was postponed and later held in November. We attended that event and got introduced to many more members of the Indian diaspora in Addis Ababa.

Even after we moved to the new house, our social circle was still limited. Partly because I was overly occupied with the coffee launch and partly because we didn't make an effort. On January 26, 2009, I and Runa went to the Indian Embassy for the flag hosting. As I was waiting for the hoisting, a middle-aged gentleman who was standing next to me started talking to me. He asked, "Are you new in Addis? where I was from in India?" I replied, "Yes, sir, I came last year. I am from Madhya Pradesh". He immediately asked, "Where in Madhya Pradesh?" I told him about a city called Indore. He was super excited to hear that and asked me, "Where do you stay in Indore?" I was surprised by that question, and I told him, "Sir, this is the first time somebody has asked me this question in Addis. Do you know Indore?" He smiled and said "Most of my life I have spent Indore, so I know Indore very well" I was very happy to hear that, and as we started talking about Indore Soon, we realized that we had a lot of common connections.

He was Mr. Sushil Dubey. He was heading the Tata International operations in Addis Ababa at that time.

Since Tata International was importing a lot of leather, he was sent to develop leather products for exports from Ethiopia and to represent Tata Group in Ethiopia. Sushil Ji's wife, Anushri Ji, is also a very sweet lady, and we quickly developed a PP partnership! This PP partnership stands for the POHA and PAKODA partnership. Any one of us making Poha or pakoda would invite the other. Since we both came from Indore, we relished the Poha. We used to catch up once a week and spend time together. Sushil ji and Anushri ji used to be great hosts, and we would have them come over to our place regularly. They stayed in Addis until much after we left, and we still shared a very strong bond.

By January 2009, I also started to go to the India Embassy with Vikash and Sanjay bhai on Sundays to play cricket. As I started to go there, I got introduced to more Indians who were in Addis for business or employment purposes. I got introduced to Rajiv Sharma, who was in the process of setting up a paper manufacturing plant in Ethiopia. Rajeev Bhai was a wonderful person, very warm and helpful. As we got to know them, his wife, Anjali Bhabhi, was also a very sweet lady. Their daughter Ragini was in the Greek Community School and would regularly check on Urvi. Besides, Rajiv Bhaiya is a wonderful singer and would make every get together so special with his songs. I also met Abhishek Bhai, who was working for a Singapore-based processed food company and was heading their Africa operations. He and his wife, Prachi, were very friendly, and Runa instantly got very close to Prachi. Their daughter Anusha had her birthday just a week before Urvi's birthday, and invariably we would have the birthday parties at the same location, one week apart.

The initiative to play at the embassy was encouraged by the then Indian Ambassador, H.E. Gurjit Singh. Amb Gurjit Singh was an astute diplomat who worked very hard to make India-Ethiopia links stronger. India-Ethiopia diplomatic relations were at their peak during his time. Though he was an avid cricket fan, he rarely got time to be there on Sundays. But other members of the Embassy staff, Dr. Rajesh Ranjan, Naveen Sharma ji, Subhash Chand Ji, Rajneesh Singh, and the security attaché Sheesham, As I started playing cricket on Sundays, my bond with all of them developed. Soon our families also started to join in, and the women would spend time together socializing, playing badminton, or chitchatting. Slowly, I and Runa started to enjoy our social life in Addis and look forward to Sundays every week.

Quite often, it is said that the officers in the Indian missions abroad are very high-headed. We found the absolute reverse. We got introduced to almost everyone at the Indian embassy. I found them all to be very polite and genuine people. Dr. Rajesh Ranjan, the first Secretary, and his wife Upma were a very gracious couple. They would be very participative in all the functions, and one would enjoy their company. Their daughter was about the same age as Urvi, and in her, Urvi found great company in Addis. Subhash Chand was the second secretary at the embassy and was very soft-spoken. His wife, Raman Chand, was also a fun-loving person, and it would be an absolute pleasure to be with them. Their sons, Sagar and Saarash, were quite witty and would always be up to something exciting. Naveen Sharma and his wife Nishi

Sharma made up a very cheerful couple and would add a lot of humour to the discussions. Their daughters, Nikita and Divya, like their parents, were very humble and fun-loving. For about a year, Rajnish Singh was also there in the embassy. Rajnish and his wife Anjali had two sons, Shashank and Vikramank. Rajneesh was a person you would enjoy talking to for hours. Soon Rajnish left and was replaced by a joyful couple, Davinder and Manju Singh. Davinder was a bundle of energy, and Manju was very calm and stable. Together, they made a great couple. Both worked for the MEA, the government of India. Also, as Dr. Ranjan left Addis, Mr. Srinivasan and Angha joined, along with their son and daughter. They were also very hospitable, and we had several get-togethers at their place as well. In my opinion, most of the staff that was in the Indian Embassy in Addis Ababa was, by far, very humble and down to earth, including Ambassador Gurjit Singh.

As our social circle increased, we also got introduced to the Mukherjee family—Udyan and Rajshree Mukherjee. Though they were comparatively senior to us, they were younger than us when it came to hearts. Rajshree Bhabhi was a renowned singer, and we would look forward to listening to her at any event. Udyan Mukherjee was heading the operations of a company called OIA, which was redeveloping several sugar mills in Ethiopia with the government of India's support. He was very down-to-earth and a very helpful person. We also got introduced to Dr Umesh and Nilima Kadam. Umesh Ji was working for the ICCR and was based in Addis Ababa. He was a prolific writer and had written several books. Meeting him used to be a very educational experience, as he had so many stories to tell. Through Sanjay Bhai, I was also introduced to Shailesh Maniar. He was running a plastic manufacturing unit in Ethiopia. He introduced us to Marsila's Pizzeria, which was our favourite place for Pizza in Addis. Shailesh Ji helped me a lot when I was winding up from Addis. He helped me get the shipping company to ship my goods back. Due to some confusion, the stuff remained with the shipper, and later, Shailesh Ji helped me recover it. Another family we made very good friends with was the Gautams- Naresh and Chandni.

During that time, under the diplomatic arrangement, a group of Indian Army officers were also in Addis. The team was led by Col. Rahul Singh, with his wife Mrs Ritu Singh and son, and several other officers were in Addis. We also got introduced to them. The local Indian community in Addis was also reasonably large. As our social circle expanded, we met friends like Mayur and Rupal Kothari. Mayur Bhai and Rupal Bhabhi were a wonderful couple, a wonderful host, and very down-to-earth and humble people. Their son, Harsh, was studying in London and is now back in Addis Ababa. I connected with him much later, but I found him to be a wonderful person. While in Addis, I also got introduced to some other very good friends who worked in the developmental sector, Sunil Awasthi ji and Pankaj Bhai. They are still very good friends. In 2022, when I travelled to Bangladesh, I was able to catch up with Pankaj Bhai, who showed the same warmth as we had when we were in Addis. Meeting Sunil Awasthi ji is still pending, and I look forward to it eagerly.

Runa was enjoying teaching at the Indian National School. As part of the school's annual celebrations, she also organized a play about a pencil and a mouse. Both characters were played by children of known families who were also students at the Indian National School. This became very popular as all the props were made internally in the school, and it was the first time such a play was done. Pencil was played by Davya, daughter of our friend Satish Vuyuyur. Satish is a wonderful person, having his business in Ethiopia. He runs a packaging company, and the paper to make the pencil prop came from him. The mouse was played by a student, who was also the son of Runa's colleague. Runa, by now, was very comfortable, had even picked up Amharic, and could speak more Amharic than me.

When I joined the UNDP, as part of the UN relocation support, I was allowed to import household stuff, including a car, for our personal use. Since I had already rented a fully furnished house, I did not require any other furnishing to be brought in, but I definitely required a car. Cars in Ethiopia were very expensive because of the high import duty. I, as an UNDP employee, was given tax-free car importation rights. My office colleagues Solomon and Ahadu were importing all the household furniture and fixtures, along with a car. There was an opportunity for me to import a car with them at a shared cost. I went to Dubai in October 2008 to buy a car. This was my first time in Dubai, and buying a car in Dubai was itself a wonderful experience. I bought a white Toyota Corolla car, and the agents shipped it to me to reach somewhere in mid-November 2008. Since it was registered under a UN quote, the car carried a UN number plate, and that would be a proud feeling for me driving it.

I required the car to be used for Runa and Urvi as well; I was looking for a driver. I was introduced to Antenna by the son of a driver from the exchange. He would drive us every morning, where we would first drop Urvi off at the school, then drop Runa off at the Indian National School, and finally, Anthenna would drive me to my office. Afternoon, he would go pick up Urvi from her school and then pick up Runa and drive them home. He was very particular about timing and made sure that he was never late so that Urvi wouldn't have to wait in the school. Sometimes when I was out with him, he would tell me that I should pack up early because he has to go and pick up Urvi. I was very comfortable, as Anthenna was a trustworthy and honest person. Also, after the initial language problems with the maid, we got a wonderful girl, Kadijah. We were still in the apartment, and she would go and pick up Urvi from school. Since it was walking distance, we were comfortable. However, she got a job in the Middle East and left. In our new house, we found another very nice maid, Naijat. She worked with us until our last day in Addis.

Like every year, in 2009 also, the embassy was planning the Diwali function. Amb. Gurjit Singh had moved, and Dr. Rajesh Ranjan was the acting ambassador. It was decided that different dances would be presented by different groups, representing the cultures of India. Naveen ji called ten of us to suggest that we present a bhangra on that day. I had never performed a dance on stage, but nevertheless, with everybody around me, I readily agreed. We practiced for close to two months, and our trainers were Jaswinder Singh, or Jassi, as we called him, and a 10th grade student, Aftab Chawla, or

Abu, as he was known. Aftab's parents, Dr. Chawla and Neena Chawla, were also our friends in Addis. Aftab was the younger son staying with them in Addis, whereas the elder son was in India. Both Dr. Chawla and Neena Chawla were wonderful couple. Neena Ji was a wonderful cook as well. Unfortunately, some years ago, Aftab passed away in an accident. After our return from Addis, we had visited them in Ludhiana, and that was last we saw Aftab.

Jassi and Abu were both very good at dance and then guided us for the dance practice. We worked really hard and prepared the best dance we could. Naveen ji also arranged the costume from India, and on the Diwali day celebration, we were all dressed up in traditional Punjabi dancer outfits to present at the dance in front of the audience. I don't know about the audience, but I thoroughly enjoyed it. The video of this performance is still there on YouTube. In the same event, Runa and her friends performed a Rajasthani dance. From 2008 Diwali, when we were just new to Addis, to 2009 Diwali, we had settled down and were enjoying our social lives in Addis Ababa.

In 2009, we also had our first mega celebration in Addis Ababa. It was Urvi's birthday, and we decided to celebrate it on a grand scale, as by then we had a big social circle in Addis. We wanted to invite everyone and have a fun-filled evening. As a sahajayogi, I cannot, should not, and do not consume liquor or even serve it at my house or at celebrations. The celebration was planned at the De Leopold hotel, and we went to meet the chef, Mohan. Just a day before, we had been there to celebrate Abhishek Bhai's daughter's first birthday, and it was a lot of fun. We decided to have the party there and met Mohan to discuss the details. We finalized the menu, and when the question of liquor came, Mohan asked me if, since I work for the UN and get subsidized liquor, I would be bringing my own or if he had to arrange it. I told him that at this celebration, no liquor would be served. He was taken aback, and he said this was not possible. All the guests would ask me for liquor. What will we do? Then he said we would put beer bottles along with cold drinks that might be okay. I said not even beers but only cold drinks would be served, and if anybody has any problems, they should talk to me. I know he was not comfortable with that proposition, and he was sceptical about the party. To his surprise, none of our friends missed the alcohol, and everybody enjoyed the party to the fullest. This is what friendship is! Everybody knew that we do not serve or drink alcohol, and everyone, respecting our sentiments and beliefs, did not feel absence of alcohol as a party spoiler. Everyone was comfortable without alcohol and had a wonderful time. This made me respect my friends more than earlier.

By 2009, Runa's brother Amit had also joined us in Addis Ababa. Amit was looking for a job, and I was told that one of our friends, Shyam Bhai, was looking for an accountant in his company. I introduced him to Amit, and he felt that Amit would be a suitable candidate. Amit was selected, and he relocated to Addis Ababa to work with Shyam Bhai's company. Amit stayed in Addis for about a year, after which he started to experience problems. His salary was not being paid regularly, and I had to intervene and request that Shyam bhai release his salary. Amit is shy by nature and would find it very difficult to argue for his salary. Not to doubt Shyam Bhai's intentions, as the business was also under financial constraint and was not doing as well as it should have been, the salary still remained unpaid for a long period. In April 2011, Amit returned to India as he was tired of working in Addis.

In November 2009, one evening, Sushil Dubey ji called us for dinner. It was a weekday, and when we turned up, he introduced me to a smart young man, saying he was Captain Sachin More. I thought Sachin was part of the military delegation that was based in Addis. Sachin corrected me and said he was with the Indian army earlier, is now retired, and is working with the EXIM Bank of India. The EXIM Bank of India was planning to open a branch in Addis Ababa. He had come to do the groundwork for the opening, and Sushil Ji was a connection that he was relying upon. As we got introduced, Sachin and I started to get along very nicely. I started to give him all the information he required and advice that I could for his work in Addis Ababa. I could see he was listening to my advice as he found it relevant to his work. He relocated to Addis Ababa in 2010, and in September 2010, the official opening of the EXIM Bank of India's office happened. After that, Sachin and I would often catch up. Sachin became the third member of our PP partnership with Dubey Ji. It would be me, Sachin and Dubey ji getting together more often apart from the bigger group where all of us would be there.

Sachin was a wonderful human being but a very strict administrator. He was a no-nonsense guy and would develop social contacts and relationships very carefully. He was very careful about his and his organization's image and would not, in any way, want to compromise with that image. In September 2010, when Sachin was working on the inauguration event for the EXIM Bank's office, which was to be presided over by the then banking secretary, on the evening before the event, he called me a bit stressed. He said he needs help arranging a car for his delegation from India. The embassy had arranged the car, but only for the banking secretary. He needs a car for the CMD of EXIM Bank. The car has to be at least a Mercedes, and he was not able to find one. I gave him the contact details of my friend in the UN, who was the protocol officer and was in charge of arranging all these vehicles for the UN delegations. He immediately connected Sachin with the right vendors for the car. Within an hour, his problem was solved, and I was particularly happy that I was able to help Sachin.

Whenever I visited Addis until 2012, I would stay at Sachin's place, and he would be very happy hosting me. When he returned to India, we would regularly catch up and meet occasionally. Sachin got married in 2015, and I and Dubey Ji were the only friends from Addis who were present in Mumbai. Unfortunately, after a year, Sachin passed away due to cardiac arrest, something that I cannot come to terms with even today. I and Sachin had a very special bond and a very strong trust between each other. He had been a big help to me when I was establishing my consulting business after moving out of the UN. His death is more than a personal tragedy to me.

My memories with Sachin go back to 2010, when he and I were given the responsibility to host the mega event on the Diwali occasion. That year, Amb. Bhagwant

Singh Bishnoi was posted as the Ambassador of India to Ethiopia, and it was his first Diwali celebration. He wanted to have it on a grand scale. Prior to Diwali, the Indian Women's Association planned a Dussehra function, where it was planned that Ramayana would be played as a dance drama. Khushali Vaghela, a dance teacher in Addis who used to conduct dance classes at the Indian embassy, was given the role of training the children for the dance. Runa was given the responsibility to make props for the dance drama. Runa made props for the hut using the waste material that was discarded by the Embassy during the renovation process. However, some misunderstandings got created, and Madam Rupa Bishnoi, the wife of the Indian ambassador, was very upset with Runa for reasons still unknown to Runa. She was also upset with Khushali, and that resulted in the cancellation of the Dussehra celebrations that were planned. Mrs Dubey and Raman Bhabhi tried very hard to calm things down, as no one wanted the children to be disappointed. Mrs. Bishnoi had already made up her mind, and the Dussehra celebrations were called off. It was agreed that the dance drama would be added to the Diwali celebrations so that the children would not be punished.

For the 2010 Diwali celebrations at the embassy, it was me and Sachin who were given the responsibility to host the function. This, I guess, was much easier to do than the dance we did last year, at least for me. I and Sachin prepared a detailed script and hosted the Diwali celebration among seven hundred Indians at the embassy premises. It was a lot of fun being on stage. I and Sachin thoroughly enjoyed doing that, though initially Sachin was not interested. I told him "I said that I would be there to handle everything; you just be on the stage". He was then comfortable with it and agreed to it. That is one of my most cherished memories of Sachin. We had a blast that day, and it was as if everything came naturally to us. The thing that upset me, Sachin, and a lot of other friends was what the ICCR had done.

ICCR, or Indian Centre for Cultural Relations, is an agency of the Ministry of Tourism, Government of India, that promotes Indian cultural relations across the globe. Under the name of Indian cultural relations, a dance troupe was sent to Addis Ababa to perform. This dance troop was a typical Bollywood dance troupe that was presenting Bollywood songs and dances to the audience. Now that the Diwali celebrations were connected with Indian culture, all performed by amateurs, they were still high on dignity. The Bollywood dance troop, with its item song-type dances, was not fitting in. Since they had been sent by the government of India, we had very little choice. When I was discussing this with Sachin, I suggested we have performances by the amateur Indians in Addis before the Bollywood show begins. The performers had prepared for several cultural dances that were true representations of Indian culture. I and Sachin were in no mood to spoil the sanctity of an Indian cultural event by adding a Bollywood tadka to it. We proposed that the first half of the program be hosted by us and include performances by Indians in Addis Ababa. Later on, we will hand over the stage to the Bollywood performance troupe, who can present their show to the audience. This got the approval of Mrs. Bishnoi as well. The 2010 Diwali celebration was one of the best Diwali celebrations done by the Indian Embassy till then.

This event was particularly important for me because in the audience was my mother, who had travelled all the way from India on her first international trip. It was with her determination and strong willpower that she made the journey from Indore to Mumbai and from Mumbai to Addis, with all the travel challenges, without any complaint. We were lucky as Mr. and Mrs Dubey were also traveling on the same flight, and they could help my mother if required. Since I was an UN employee with a diplomatic ID, I could go up to the immigration counter to receive my mother. She came to Addis in August and stayed with her till the end of October. As my mother was in town, every one of our close friends, like Rajiv bhaiya, Abhishek bhaiya, Subhash Ji, Naveen Ji, and Dubey Ji, invited us for dinner. It was a particularly enjoyable time, and my mother was also very comfortable with the social settings. She also attended my daughter's birthday, which we organized in a similar fashion to last year. In 2010, my office colleagues also joined me. 2010 was a particularly important year for me. That year, I had completed my PhD and also published two books

There are a lot of memories from Addis Ababa's social life that I still cherish. Celebrating the World Cup 2011 triumph, celebrating various festivals like Holi, Diwali, and others, even Lohdi together with friends, the picnics to Kuriftu, Langano, and Havassa, and many other memories On the 5th of August 2011, we had a big celebration, which was our farewell to our friends in Addis Ababa. This farewell dinner was especially emotional for us, and on that evening, I and Runa remembered what Dr. Sharma had told us: that when the time to go from Ethiopia came, you would cry! And we really cried that night, as our stay in Ethiopia is now over. On August 8, 2011, Runa and Urvi left for India, and a week later I left for my first US visit, winding up our lives in Addis Ababa.

CHAPTER THIRTEEN

New Life, Own Master

By late 2010, the ECX had started to become more and more profitable as commodity volumes kept increasing. By the end of February 2011, the ECX had celebrated the Thousand Day-One Billion celebration, indicating that Ethiopia had touched a trading volume of one billion US dollars, which was by no means a small achievement. Ethiopia's commodity Exchange was becoming more and more prominent in the world and was getting recognition across the globe. Since 2009, several dignitaries have visited the ECX, which has put the exchange on the global map. The hard work put in by the team since 2008 has made it a benchmark for commodity exchanges in Africa.

In 2009, PBS wanted to make a video story on how Ethiopia is building its commodity exchange and how the commodity exchange is going to transform the lives of millions of farmers in Ethiopia. The Public Broadcasting Service (PBS) is an American public broadcaster and free-to-air television network based in Arlington, Virginia. They run a documentary program named Wide Angle.

This story was to be part of the Wide-Angle program. They came to Ethiopia and eventually decided that the story should be made about the efforts of Dr. Eleni to develop the commodity exchange in Ethiopia. Eventually, when the story came out, it became more of a Dr. Eleni story than an ECX story.

Dr. Eleni was also enjoying the limelight she was getting from the success of the ECX. The success of the ECX had led to a rush in African countries to set up their own commodity exchanges. Suddenly, in the donor community and government circles, this became a must-do project. Many countries had approached the ECX for support and knowledge sharing. Numerous delegations had visited the ECX to understand how Ethiopians are doing the commodity exchange business and how it can be replicated. This rush was not only in African countries; I remember a delegation coming all the way from the Philippines. They wanted to start a rice exchange in the Philippines and came to Ethiopia to see what was happening and how it was making the trade successful.

This whole thing—the media and the public's attention—was a different experience than the experience up until now. The exchange had now become properly rooted in terms of its operations, technology, and market. Increasing volumes of commodities started to come in, and the exchange was becoming successful by all parameters. The interesting thing was that the efforts required to be put in on business development were not really very high, as the ECX was getting business because of the government proclamation in coffee, sesame, and white pea beans. Apart from these three and the one

World Food Program procurement drive, beyond that, not much had happened on the exchange. But these three commodities were successfully transacted, and it was enough to show the world what changes the exchange is bringing to the lives of millions of farmers.

Since the ECX was now on autopilot mode, it was decided by Dr. Eleni that the management teams needed to be restructured and we needed to bring in a different structure for the exchange. I must confess that these changes were not discussed in the management team meeting, at least not in any one where I was present. The decision was directly conveyed by Dr. Eleni about the changes made. This meant that the new roles were defined and the department was reorganized. Under the new role, Ben was given the responsibility of chief strategy officer(CSO) and was made responsible for strategy, business development, marketing, and new products. Solomon was given the responsibility of being the CIO, and everything related to technology and hardware was his responsibility. He had recently won the CIO of Africa award as well. Dr. Kadri, though, continued to work as chief risk officer; his powers were given to other local officers. Keith, who had resigned earlier, was retained as a consultant, and the responsibility of the central depository function, along with clearing and settlement, was given to Ahadu. Ahadu was made the COO of the exchange, with everything related to operations falling under his control. At the same time, Aman was given the responsibility of being the CBO of the exchange, and he continued to look after the warehouse operations and warehouse functions.

As far as my new role was concerned, I was designated as the Chief Economist, and a new function was added. This was research, publications, and training. The focus on training was put on this because Dr. Eleni realized that a lot of commodity exchange initiatives in Africa are looking for technical support from the ECX, and this training department would be the ideal choice for the exchange to offer such technical trainings. She asked me to develop a concept paper and a proposal for the establishment of the ECX Institute, which would be the institute that handles everything related to foreign collaborations, technological collaborations, and trainings for new and upcoming commodity exchange initiatives.

For me and many in the team, the reorganization of the department was confusing, more in reference to the timing of it. Within the government, the discussion was on the transfer of operational control to the locally recruited team and the international technical experts, that is, Dr. Eleni and her team, to phase out the exchange. The government had initially agreed with the UNDP and other donors that support would be available for the government and the ECX for an initial three years. Within these three years, the local capacities were to be developed, and the local staff was to be prepared to hand over control of the exchange. This was applicable to the CEO and all the departmental heads. So, on the one hand, when the government was preparing for the phasing out of key expatriate staff, this type of change did not make sense, at least to me. There may have been a thought process, which I was not privy to, that might have resulted in this restructuring.

Dr. Eleni was opposing the government's decision and saying that it would take one more year for the exchange to develop local capacities and local staff to take over commodity exchange management. The UNDP perks to the exchange staff were widely complained about, especially by the other government companies, who considered ECX to be at par with them. Due to this, the pressure on the government was high to end the UNDP engagement. Our status was unique in Ethiopia; in spite of being UNDP staff, we were operating as government of Ethiopia staff for them. For the Government of Ethiopia, we were being paid as UNDP staff, being government staff. This was not comfortable for either the government or the UNDP.

By then, governments seemed to be adamant on their initial plan, and the compromise reached was that there would be a six-month extension given, beyond which control of the exchange would be handed over to the locally recruited staff. This was again opposed by Dr. Eleni, and the final proposal she put forward to the government was to retain half of the management team for the full year rather than retaining the full management team for half of the year. This was agreed upon by the government, and it was decided that half of the management team would phase out on completion of their three years in August. The remaining half would continue to train the local staff and hand over control of the exchange to the local staff by the end of the next six months. This way, by March 2012, it was expected that the exchange would be handed over to the local management team. The decision on who would phase out when was not yet taken, and the decision was left on Dr. Eleni to look at the operational challenges and decide. The lack of clarity on who is going to be retained and who will be phased out in August created a lot of uncertainty among the management team. However, a lot of people felt that the way the reorganization of the Exchange management was done, Dr. Eleni already picked the people to be retained.

Dr. Eleni was continuing her outreach to the continent as the negotiations with the government were going on. In an effort to strengthen the relationship between the ECX and the new African commodity exchange initiatives, Dr. Eleni organized a forum in the end of February 2011 in Addis Ababa. This was jointly organized with several donors, who were happy to support the ECX in inviting other African commodity exchange initiatives for discussion. This forum was organized by Dr. Eleni to put the ECX in the leadership role for commodity exchange establishment in Africa and see how many new initiatives in Africa would like to replicate and learn from the ECX. The forum received a good response, and a lot of initiatives turned up for it. The thought that Dr. Eleni was propagating was that Africa needs an African way to establish a commodity exchange. In attendance was another stalwart in the commodity exchange sector in India, the former head of SAFEX, Rod Boldin.

When this question was presented by Dr. Eleni to Rod, he disagreed, and from the podium, he said that there is a right way or a wrong way to do a commodity exchange. There cannot be an African way to do a commodity exchange separately. Whatever we are doing is what the world has done, and based on the lessons learned by the world, we can do the right thing or the wrong thing. This comment particularly did not go down well with Dr. Eleni, who wanted to put forward to the African Community that the right way of doing the commodity exchange is the Ethiopian way. I also participated in this forum and was able to develop a lot of relationships with various African initiatives that were looking for experts who could do the same thing in their country. I was not aware by then that this would lead to being believed to be a competition with Dr. Eleni!

One of the relationships I developed was with Godfrey Malekano, who was the commodity exchange project leader in Tanzania. He was working for the Capital Market and Securities Authority of Tanzania, and the government of Tanzania had tasked the authority to set up a commodity exchange in Tanzania. They were working on this project. I interacted with Godfrey and gave him a lot of input on what they could do to develop a commodity exchange in Tanzania. He was very interested in what I was saying, and he asked me if I could come over to Tanzania to talk to the government and make a presentation. I said I would be happy, and we can discuss the modalities. Little did I know that this would be something that would lead to a lot of confusion and misunderstandings at the ECXs.

I travelled to India at the end of March to speak at the India-Africa Project Partnership summit, organized by the Confederation of Indian Industries and EXI Bank of India. At the summit, I spoke about the commodity exchange as a solution to a lot of food security problems, and alongside me on the panel was the agriculture minister of Malawi, Hon. Peter Mwanza. After the session, when we interacted, I told him, "Sir, I know that India imports about hundred thousand tons of pigeon peas from Malawi." He immediately asked me, "Then where does the money go? I was not prepared, and I told him, "Sir, it is for you to find out, and that is the exact reason why you need structured markets in Malawi that could help your government in tracking the trades and, more importantly, tracking the revenues that the country is generating."

This statement became very relevant to me in the upcoming days of my career, as eventually I worked in Malawi as well. After this summit, while returning from India, the Tanzanians asked me if I could stop over in Tanzania and make a presentation to the Tanzanian stakeholders on the concept of commodity exchange. It was to be a very generic presentation, and I did not see anything wrong with it. I readily agreed, and on my way to Ethiopia during my official leave, I went to Tanzania to make a presentation on the concept of the commodity exchange. After this presentation was made over lunch, the representative from the president's office was very keen and asked me if I could make a presentation for the President. It was a big occasion for me, and I said I would be very happy to do that. On my return to Ethiopia, I went to Dr. Eleni and requested a clarification about my role at the ECX after August 2011, as half of us had to phase out. I was keen to know if I would be retained or asked to leave, as it was not clear. In the discussion, Dr. Eleni did not give me any clear ideas. I asked a different question "In that case, should I start looking for options after August?" and she said, "It's always good to have options in your hand." I took it as her concurrence to me looking at other options after August 2011 inside as well as outside the United Nations Development Program.

After getting an indication from Dr. Eleni that I should be looking at other options after August, I started looking for the same. Some opportunities in UNDP were there, but I was interested in doing something I had started to like: commodity exchange development. I responded to an email from my newly developed connections in Tanzania, who were keen to know if I would be available after August to help them build a similar exchange in Tanzania. I indicated that I would be happy to discuss the modalities of an assignment after my assignment with the ECX is over. By then, I was prepared to leave the United Nations Development Program if an equally lucrative opportunity was offered. The Tanzanian team consulted with the President, and on the President's instruction, I was invited to make a presentation to the President in Cape Town, on the side-lines of the World Economic Forum for Africa.

I was told that if the President is convinced by the proposition and the model that I are proposing, then the government of Tanzania would be keen to discuss with me an engagement for Tanzania. At this point in time, there was nothing guaranteed and nothing agreed upon. I considered this a presentation for a job interview, where I had to convince my future recruiters that I understood the subject matter sufficiently and had the capacity to deliver what they were looking for. I was called to Cape Town to make the presentation. For me to go to Cape Town, I decided to take a leave and do this presentation in my personal time. Dr. Eleni was not in office that week and had given the charge to Ahadu to take decisions in her absence. I informed him that I would not be available next week and would be on leave as I would be traveling. He advised me to drop an email to Dr. Eleni, and if she has any reservations, she would respond back. I understood that if she does not respond with an objection, my leave is sanctioned and I can go ahead and make the presentation. I dropped the required email, and as I did not receive any objections from Dr. Eleni, I decided to go to Johannesburg and then Cape Town to make the presentation.

In Cape Town, I was greeted by the team from the President's office and made the presentation for the President. The President had invited various stakeholders to that meeting, and representatives from different organizations like the World Bank, the Bill and Melinda Gates Foundation, USAID, UNDP, and many other organizations were present. After the presentation, I was approached by many people who represented many sectors. There were investors, traders, development partners, and government representatives. I don't remember who, but someone from one of the donor agencies, approached me. When I told him about working with the ECX, he asked me, Why didn't Dr. Eleni come? To this, I answered that because I was invited, I came. It was a very casual discussion for both of us, and I did not see anything serious in it.

When I reached Addis Ababa on May 6, 2011, on Friday night, I didn't suspect any problems. By Sunday, I started to know that Dr. Eleni was trying to look for me and find out where I was. Apparently somebody whom she knew was attending the presentation in Cape Town and asked her why I was representing ECX and not she? This, in my opinion, was a misunderstanding, as I was not representing ECX but presenting a concept of commodity exchange to the President of Tanzania for his consideration and opinions on replicating it in Tanzania. However, the question created a misunderstanding.

As I heard about it, I was not sure why Eleni was looking for me, and I decided that when I went to work on Monday, I would personally ask her and discuss it with her. I wanted to share with her the information that I had been to Johannesburg and Cape Town to make a presentation as I was invited by the president, who is considering hiring me for the development of the commodity exchange in Tanzania. By then, Dr. Eleni had focused her attention on looking for consulting opportunities where ECX or Dr. Eleni could step in and undertake consulting assignments for setting up commodity exchanges. She saw my initiative as a competition to hers and was not amused by that.

As this was unfolding, another thing happened that created more confusion and misunderstandings. When I was in India for the Confederation of Indian Industries-EXIM Bank Summit, I was contacted by an officer from the Ethiopian Embassy, who introduced me to a journalist, Ishani Duttagupta from the Economic Times. The journalist was looking for Indians who have done some phenomenal work out of India, and in the opinion of the Ethiopian Embassy, I had done pretty interesting work with the ECX. Since India and Ethiopia relations were very strong and the next India-Africa Forum

Summit was to be held in Addis Ababa, they thought this would be a good idea to promote and highlight India's support for Ethiopia by popularizing the story of an Indian going to Ethiopia to help ECXs get established.

This was something they wanted to highlight in this interview. They introduced me to Ishani, and I readily agreed to the interview, and the interview was done. This actually got published only on Sunday, May 8, 2011, when I had just returned from Johannesburg. The title of the article that was published in the Economic Times on May 8th (Electronic version) said, "***How Kulkarni designed the first ECX in Africa.***" This link was shared with Dr. Eleni by someone, and it added to the confusion and misunderstanding that I was trying to compete with Dr. Eleni in setting up commodity exchanges and that I was trying to steal the credit for developing the commodity exchange in Ethiopia. Up until now, most of the publications said that it was Dr. Eleni who developed the commodity exchange in Ethiopia; this one presented my name. It is my strong belief that, though the leadership was that of Dr. Eleni and a lot of strategic decisions were taken by her, it was a team effort that built the ECX. The exchange became what it was because each individual contributed to its fullest capacity and made sure that the exchange was successful and became an institution of excellence.

All these misunderstandings and confusions led to a very angry approach from Dr. Eleni, who decided that I had crossed the line by going to Tanzania. This led to her filing a complaint against me with the United Nations Development Program, accusing me of sabotaging the ECX and trying to align with a different government using government of Ethiopia resources. I very strongly opposed these accusations and put forward my case very convincingly that it was not the intention, but an effort to secure an assignment after my assignment at the ECX is finished. Even the Tanzanians vouched for the same and confirmed to me in writing that I was not involved in any government or private project in Tanzania, and my presentation was only a part of our ongoing discussions for an assignment after August 2011.

I was able to convince the UNDP disciplinary committee, which found no evidence of any wrongdoing on my part. After a detailed investigation, it was concluded that there was no evidence that could link my involvement with the Tanzanian project to sabotage of the ECX. However, this meant that my name was at the top of the list of the technical experts who would finish their assignment by August 2011 and not continue beyond that. I, Aman, and Dr. Kadri were the three officers who moved out of the ECX in August 2011, ending our very successful engagement with the exchange, where we helped Ethiopia build a world-class exchange that was becoming an African benchmark. I still believe that the Tanzania misunderstanding was a smoke screen, and the die was already cast for three of us in January 2011, when the reorganization happened.

When I look back at the work that I have done I feel proud that most of the work that I did in Ethiopia is now becoming a best practice to be followed by many upcoming exchanges. My contribution to the ECX started when it was a concept and ended when it had become an African benchmark of success and many African countries were looking at the ECX to learn and replicate for them. This is particularly the most satisfying part of the journey that I was able to contribute to build such a successful institution in Ethiopia. In the process I also learnt a lot of things that still are important for me and help me in my work event today. The journey of the ECX for me was no less than a fairy tale and I decided that now after my assignment at the ECX is over, I would not continue with UNDP, rather would like to build my own consulting firm, that can work on setting up the commodity exchanges in Africa and outside. I was keen to work on the overall agricultural value chains. That time, UNDP had shortlisted me for some of the projects. But the choice was between a cosy UNDP life or doing something that I would love to do. I consulted my wife and she suggested take a decision that will make you happy. That was the time when I moved out of UNDP and started working on developing my consulting firm the Stalwart Management Consultancy Services. A new life, where I would be my own master had started. Immediately after my assignment was over with UNDP in Addis Ababa, I flew for a three-week tour to the United States of America and when I returned, I was clear where I want to take my life. It was time for me to start a New Life with being own master.

Epilogue

I ended my assignment at the ECX with a determination to build my own consulting firm and establish myself as a consultant in the field of structured markets and value chains in Africa. After about twelve years of my work, today I can say that I have established what I wanted to when I moved out of the ECX. My moving out of the ECX was a decision that was already made with the government's decision to retain only half of the management team and phase the remaining management team off by August 2011. In any case, I had gone to Ethiopia with a time horizon of five months and ended up staying close to four years, building the world-class commodity exchange in Ethiopia.

I am still proud of the work that I have been doing and the features that I have brought to the exchange. May It be the warehouse base contracts, which have become a template for all the exchanges in Africa, or the standardization of hundreds of types of coffee into less than fifty, or may it be designing the futures and forward strategy for the ECX, which eventually in 2022-2023 is being implemented, I feel that I have significantly contributed to the process of making the exchange what it is today. When I look back, I feel there are four corners to the whole story of the ECX. It is me, Dr. Eleni, my colleagues, and the exchange itself. After August 2011, all four corners started their own independent journeys, and everyone has achieved phenomenal success in whatever they did.

Coming back to my story, after leaving the ECX and the United Nations Development Program, I went to the USA for three weeks, where I spoke at Penn State University. That three-week period gave me a lot of opportunity to think and decide my course of action for establishing my consulting business. The first project I got was in Ethiopia itself. I was asked to help the Shapoorji Pallonji group develop a strategy for the agriculture trade for their farm in Ethiopia. It was an opportunity that put me straight in contact with Cyrus Mystery, who was the Managing Director of the Shapoorji Pallonji Group. At that point in time, we worked on the strategy and presented it to him as a detailed finding report, which he appreciated. I remember him allocating us only twenty minutes for the presentation initially, and after ten minutes into the presentation, he asked his executive assistant to cancel his appointment for the next two hours as he would like to listen and discuss our presentation. It was indeed a recognition of our capabilities and the quality of the work that we had done.

I and my former colleague, Yohannes Assafa, started working together on commodity exchange consulting. We worked together on the feasibility study in Tanzania for a commodity exchange. By 2012, most of my time was consumed in Malawi, where I was able to build a similar exchange like Ethiopia from end-to-end. My interactions with the Malawians started after I met the minister in March 2011 in India and finally moved for a long-term period to Malawi in February 2012 for the next two years. I built a commodity exchange in Malawi with my colleague and dear friend, Dr Niraj Vijyvergiya, and handed it over to the local staff for management in 2014.

I also got the honor in Rwanda, as the finance minister of Rwanda appointed me as an adviser for the commodity market's master-planned development. I and Yohannes did the feasibility study for Kenya as well. Later, I also worked in Ghana, Egypt, Nigeria, and even Bangladesh and Nepal. I continue to work in the commodity exchange sector and have achieved phenomenal success in the development of commodity exchanges in this region. More than five commodity exchanges that have been up in Africa have had my contribution in some way or another. With fifteen countries and twenty five projects successfully completed in Africa since 2011, I feel the decision I took was vindicated.

Dr. Eleni had also planned to do a similar thing and, since 2012, has been trying to get into the consulting business for the commodity exchanges. Our paths crossed in Tanzania, where she was initially invited. However, for some reasons unknown to me, the Tanzanians decided to work with us, and we were given the assignment to do the feasibility study. Dr. Eleni wanted to work in Tanzania but could not have a lot of success. She also went to Rwanda with Amb. Jendayi Frazer, who was an American diplomat in Africa and now is a developmental investor. Jendayi had a commodity exchange project in mind for Rwanda, but soon Dr. Eleni and Jendayi fell apart. Dr. Eleni could not work in Rwanda, and Jendayi called us to work on the project. We had deployed a team of four technical experts in Rwanda.

Dr. Eleni had established a company in 2013, which was called Eleni Exchanges, and the idea she was bringing to the table was a turnkey solution for commodity exchange establishment. She had also gotten committed financing from IFC, Bob Geldof's Eight mile Fund, and Morgan Stanley. However, her investors quickly wore out and pulled out of the investment. The little bit of traction that Dr. Eleni could gather in the commodity exchange segment was in Ghana, where she worked for a while for the establishment of the Ghana commodity exchange. Subsequently, the project was handed over to local Ghanaian consultants to establish the exchange. The founder and CEO of the Ghana commodity exchange was Dr. Kadri Alfah, who coincidentally was our colleague from Ethiopia.

Dr. Eleni's company Eleni Exchanges, as a company, could not gather significant business and had tough times. I believe Dr. Eleni is now working into innovation and start-ups in Africa. I must appreciate that she has a very keen eye for the changes in trends and is always able to take decisions that help her ride the trend. I hope she is able to replicate the ECX's success with her start-up company in Addis Ababa.

Talking about my colleagues, by 2014, almost everybody from the exchange had exited. Ahadu and Solomon were still there as consultants. Solomon was building the electronic technology for the exchange and eventually was able to develop an electronic trading platform for the ECX. Subsequently, he started an IT company and did a lot of its development and installation of IT systems in Africa. He also developed the technology for the Ghana commodity exchange, and I must say it's a wonderful platform.

Yohannes and I started working together after our ECX days and eventually put a lot of work into the commodity exchange and structured markets. Even today, if an opportunity exists, we work together. Yohannes has since worked on several USAID projects and has had good success in them. Aman and Ahadu turned into entrepreneurs in Ethiopia, and both of them got into the coffee business, a sector we learned very deeply about during our exchange days. Aman has a plantation farm and exports his coffee to international markets, especially the US and Europe. He has done some pathbreaking work by setting up the first private SCAA-approved laboratory in Ethiopia; this is the first such private laboratory in Africa.

Ahadu worked for a while with the ECX and led the traceability system installation at the exchange with Solomon. Today, Ahadu is the CEO of Moyee Coffee, which is an internationally recognized coffee brand. Ben continues to work in development consulting and has done some significant projects since his exit from the ECX. Dr. Kadri served as the country representative for the East Africa exchange and then later as the founder and CEO of the Ghana commodity exchange. He has also achieved a lot of success with the Ghana commodity exchange and has built a resilient commodity exchange there.

Talking about the ECX, it continues to be the benchmark exchange in Africa. Though the exchange has lost that government support that was available until 2012, now the exchange is under a lot of pressure, and there have been times when the relevance of the exchange has been questioned. The innovation that the exchange used to bring has slowed down. In early 2023, the ECX started trading in forwards and futures, which is a welcome move at the exchange.

Looking back at our journey with the ECX, it was exciting and a learning experience. There were a lot of times when we questioned if we were doing the right thing, but the market kept telling us about our right and wrong decisions. It was an exciting and educational journey for all of us, and I believe it was because of the teamwork that the ECX was able to become such a wonderful institution.

www.ingramcontent.com/pod-product-compliance
Lightning Source LLC
LaVergne TN
LVHW100303210926
848480LV00003B/1012

* 9 7 9 8 8 9 1 3 3 3 1 3 0 *